DATE			

QUICK RESPONSE THERAPY

QUICK RESPONSE
THERAPY

A Time-Limited Treatment Approach

Judith Goldring, M.S.W.

 **HUMAN SCIENCES PRESS**

72 Fifth Avenue   3 Henrietta Street
NEW YORK, NY 10011 ● LONDON, WC2E 8LU

Copyright © 1980 by Human Sciences Press, Inc.
72 Fifth Avenue, New York, New York 10011

Printed in the United States of America
0123456789   987654321

Library of Congress Cataloging in Publication Data

Goldring, Judith.
  Quick response therapy.

  Bibliography: p. 133
  Includes index.
  1. Psychotherapy, Brief.   I. Title.
RC480.55.G64   616.89'14   LC 80-11362
ISBN 0-87705-499-1

To my father with love

CONTENTS

7

PREFACE

During my 12 years at Jewish Family Service of New York City, the period from 1972 to 1977 was spent as a supervisor of the agency's largest Quick Response unit. After I left the agency, the uniqueness and importance of this service became even more apparent to me. My purpose in this book is to introduce Quick Response in a sufficiently comprehensive way so that other professionals in other settings can learn about Quick Response treatment and about the operation of a Quick Response service. Throughout the process of writing this book, ideas have been refined, conceptual clarity enhanced, and Quick Response theory better integrated with its practice.

Quick Response* is a brief therapy developed at Jewish Family Service and used since 1971 as the modality of treatment for the majority of the agency's clients. It integrates updated concepts of when, where, and how clients need help with certain traditional principles of therapeutic intervention.

*The name "Quick Response" originated at Jewish Family Service.

Treatment starts immediately at the point of application and the practitioner who begins then with the client continues until completion of service. Time is conceived of dynamically and the time-limited nature of the client's crisis is utilized. Attention to the present aspects of the problem includes other systems within the client's environment.

Although theoretical contributions came from many disciplines, it is no accident that Quick Response was developed at Jewish Family Service. Social work's broad commitment to helping people cope with their environment involves a family agency with a wide diversity of clients, problems, and settings. This, in turn, encourages a continual synthesis of available information. A psychosocial orientation serves as an umbrella for integrating aspects of family therapy, crisis intervention, systems theory, and time-limited treatment. The spectrum of services available at Jewish Family Service reflects a comprehensive view of problems and an understanding of the range of resources needed to solve them. The Quick Response service is a product of these continual efforts to develop more effective ways of reaching out and helping people.

The book begins with the history of the movement and the theoretical principles that contributed to the development of Quick Response. All aspects of the treatment are then presented in sufficient detail to educate the reader about the clinical processes involved. Case illustrations are used extensively to bring the abstract material to life and help the reader move from theory to practice. Chapter 4 outlines the operational delivery system needed when extrapolating the treatment of one client into a functioning service for a larger agency population. Particular attention is paid in Chapter 5 to training issues for the practitioner new to Quick Response, as well as to supervisory and administrative considerations in the operation of such a service. Finally, the broad applicability of Quick Response to a wide range of clients, problems, and settings is discussed in Chapter 6.

I would like to acknowledge the important contributions

of Frances L. Beatman, Sanford N. Sherman, and Arthur L. Leader, under whose leadership Jewish Family Service began Quick Response and whose direction facilitated its growth, and of Sylvia Ross, who was Brooklyn Borough Supervisor throughout these critical years of development. I am especially grateful to all the Quick Response workers I have supervised, whose cases are presented here and from whom I have learned so much. I would like to extend special thanks to Stanley Burden, who has always encouraged me to expand myself both as a Quick Response supervisor and in writing this book, and to Dr. Herbert Strean for his support of and confidence in me throughout this project. I also wish to thank Carol Withington for her generous help with the editing of this manuscript.

Chapter 1

HISTORICAL DEVELOPMENT
AND EMERGENCE OF
QUICK RESPONSE

HISTORICAL DEVELOPMENT

Early in 1970 the administration of Jewish Family Service of New York City* decided to make what seemed at the time a radical and large-scale change in the intake practices and the number of long-term cases in the agency. The Quick Response service was instituted to provide immediate, ongoing, and time-limited treatment for the majority of the agency's clients. The practitioner who began with the client at the point of application would continue until the completion of service. Although the need for change and the direction it was to take sparked much controversy, an updated treatment modality more viable and responsive to the needs of the clients did evolve.

With hindsight, many of the elements of change can be

---

*In 1978, Jewish Family Service merged with Jewish Board of Guardians to form Jewish Board of Family And Children's Services.

clearly identified in the phenomena and direction of the 1960s. A brief review of the mood of the times in this country then, especially as social, political, and economic factors influenced mental health and social services, will help to set the stage for the development of Quick Response. The emergence of certain theoretical principles during this period was crucial to the development of new concepts of treatment and new designs for the delivery of service. By reviewing the specific intake practices of Jewish Family Service prior to 1970, practices still used by many agencies today, problem areas highlighted by the changing values and new professional concepts of the 1960s can be discussed and the importance of Quick Response put into its proper context. With this historical perspective, the principles of Quick Response will be introduced and its evolutionary, yet innovative, aspects made clearer.

Social, Political, and Economic Influences

The 1960s were a period filled with intense social activism and heightened social conscience. John F. Kennedy had ushered in the decade with his impassioned call for a renewed involvement and commitment to the kind of social change so many in our country, and especially our profession, felt was needed. With Kennedy's tragic and shocking assassination in 1963, Lyndon Johnson was given license to put the hopes and dreams of the Kennedy years into a more specific and real form. A fruitful (though short-lived) period in which money and policy were committed to bringing about changes in the area of poverty, civil rights, and education was under way. The Department of Health, Education and Welfare was given the responsibility, authority, and money to develop programs in these designated areas. In the private sector, Martin Luther King, Jr., was shifting his emphasis from the voter-registration drives in the South to the Poor People's Campaign to unite all poor people into a potent political force. For the first time the concept of disenfranchised people having their own voice in program planning emerged. Poor people no longer wanted to be "done to" but wanted a say in what was to be done.

However, the middle to late 1960s were filled with increased social conflict and turmoil over our country's involvement in Vietnam. Many people who were previously untouched by issues that would lead them to social protest felt the necessity to become involved. As the country was further torn into conflict and as the means of social protest became more determined, violence grew at home. With 1968 came the assassination of both Martin Luther King, Jr. and Robert F. Kennedy. The country was so torn and polarized over the Vietnam War that Lyndon Johnson announced he would not seek re-election. Although some of the social issues involved in the Vietnam War were the same as those central to the Civil Rights movement and the War on Poverty, this country's financial and social resources were increasingly drawn away from the concerns at home to those abroad. By the time Nixon was elected in 1968 the country was ready for his dismantling of the War on Poverty and the Civil Rights movement was about to enter a more dormant and less dramatic phase. However, this period in history had left an impact that is still evident and is still not fully understood. Its significance for the mental health profession was decisive.

The government's heavy emphasis, in terms of both energy and finances, upon programs for the poor did not go unnoticed at social service and mental health facilities. Even if poor people were not intentionally excluded, questions were now raised as to how programs were actually designed to meet the needs of these potential clients. Although a sliding fee scale might enable many clients to pay a minimum or zero fee, intake practices were in large measure still inadvertently aimed at those clients with middle-class supports and middle-class values. A minimum of attention paid to financial and concrete assistance, a waiting period for service, and the covert assumption that if clients worked hard now then changes would be realized in the future, were all consistent with a middle-class life-style (Perlman, 1965). Questions first had to be asked about the direction of the existing services before attention could be paid to finding some answers.

This intense period of social activism highlighted also the need for something other than an office-centered form of treatment. This was a time of petitions, marches, and sit-ins. Many questioned whether the practice of weekly office appointments between the professional person and client had become too customary. A tradition of social activism was interwoven in the evolution of social work and had been used from the beginning in helping the poor. While no one wished to reject the profound and significant influences of the psychoanalytic movement, social work was challenged during the 1960s to try to integrate the past and the present in a new, more dynamic way.

During this period the traditional respect shown to authority, the place the young gave to the old, and the relationship of the new to the old were all thrown into question. The election of the youngest president in our history, the challenge and defeat of the presidential authority (Johnson) that stood behind the Vietnam War indicated that the traditional hierarchical structure was losing its previously solid footing. Bureaucratic structures of all kinds were questioned and challenged. The problems of red tape and depersonalization inherent in these systems were recognized. Bigger was no longer synonymous with better and grass-root efforts were given a new place. Attention was focused on how to get around and through the bureaucratic systems that had become a part of everyone's daily life. Not only was the traditional exalted position of authority and expertise challenged, but the middle-class value of working and planning for the future came under scrutiny. The pressure that youth brought to bear on this country, the death and discrimination brought home to us by assassinations within our own boundaries and vivid pictures of the destruction of the war abroad, all contributed to a generalized questioning of our orientation to time, which so emphasized tomorrow rather than today. People were no longer quite so willing to accept the work-and-wait philosophy of the older generation.

Theoretical Principles

What did all this mean to the mental health professions? How were these societal influences actually translated into change? During the 1960s two important theories emerged and gained significant attention. Crisis theory and systems theory were a product of the times and were to shape the treatment practices being discussed here.

CRISIS THEORY.   One of the major theorists in this field, Gerald Caplan (1964), discusses the nature of crisis.

> The essential factor influencing the occurrence of crisis is an imbalance between the difficulty and importance of the problem and the resources immediately available to deal with it. The usual homeostatic, direct problem-solving mechanisms do not work, and the problem is such that other methods which might be used to sidestep it also cannot be used. In other words, the problem is one where the individual is faced by stimuli which signal danger to a fundamental need satisfaction or evoke major need appetite, and the circumstances are such that habitual problem-solving methods are unsuccessful within the time span of past expectations of success. (p. 39)

Lydia Rapoport (1965) in her classic article, "The state of crisis: Some theoretical considerations," defines a crisis state in the following terms:

> Crisis in its simplest terms is defined as "an upset in a steady state." This definition rests on the postulate that an individual strives to maintain for himself a state of equilibrium through a constant series of adaptive maneuvers and characteristic problem-solving activities through which basic need-fulfillment takes place. Throughout a life span many situations occur

which lead to sudden discontinuities by which the homeostatic state is disturbed and which result in a state of disequilibrium. In response to many such situations the individual may possess adequate adaptive or re-equilibrating mechanisms. However, in a state of crisis, by definition, it is postulated that the habitual problem-solving activities are not adequate and do not lead rapidly to the previously achieved balanced state. (p. 24)

The emergence of crisis theory during the 1960s generated a review of existing treatment practices, especially intake services. These essential points on which the new modality of treatment known as crisis intervention was based would measurably influence the direction of this review.

Most significant for our present purposes is the familiar observation that persons in crisis states are usually more ready for, and amenable to, interventive help if it is offered at the right time and at the right place; that is, during the throes of crisis before rigid defenses and related maladaptive solutions have become consolidated by the ego. Therefore, a minimal interventive force administered by a skilled person with appropriate supporting social services can produce a maximum result in a relatively short period of time. (Parad, in Parad, Ed., 1965, p. 289)

If clients request help at a point of crisis and are then most accessible, traditional intake practices had to be considered antiquated. It was no longer possible to deny availability to the client at that point; treatment had to be conceived of as beginning at application and could not be postponed by waiting periods, evaluations, and transfers that only frustrated the mental health needs of the client requesting service.

Since crisis was also considered to be "self-limiting in a temporal sense," time-limited treatment had to be considered (Caplan, 1964; Rapoport, in Parad, Ed., 1965). If the thrust of service is aimed at crisis resolution, then when this is accomplished the need for service has been met. The professional person's role is to provide temporary intervention to assist the person with his or her present difficulty and not an unfocused and generalized goal of helping him attain some "ideal image of health"(Caplan, 1964, p. 109). Research studies at this time determined that only one out of every five clients continued treatment past the fifth appointment and that the point at which termination occurred was often decided not out of a mutual plan between caseworker and client but simply by the client pulling out of treatment (Beck, 1962; Golan, 1978, p. 41). Caplan's (1964) explanation of this emphasizes the need for a treatment limited in time and focus.

> Our psychotherapeutic contact with him (client) will uncover conflicts other than those which were directly linked to his initial symptoms, and we will discover further defects in his problem solving capacity. As long as we have him in treatment, we feel that it would be valuable to help him improve in these other areas which in fact may seem more significant than the problem that first brought him to our attention. Characteristically, this leads to a psychotherapeutic process with no clear end point, treatment ends when the patient no longer wishes to continue or when the therapist's skill is no longer effective in solving his deeper problems. (p. 109)

SYSTEMS THEORY.   Along with the contributions from crisis theory, the development and prominence of systems theory during this period further facilitated an awareness of the need for change. Many saw a compatibility between the two concepts. Stein (1974) states,

> Crisis theory thus may be used as an ecological or transactional framework; it may also be used as part of general systems theory with its concept of system level hierarchy. It is amenable to various theoretical frameworks and it is typically viewed as a valuable tool in understanding and analyzing change process. (p. 69)

Gray, Duhl, and Rizzo give a basic definition of systems

theory in their introduction to *General Systems Theory and Psychiatry.*

> General systems theory may be understood from several van-
> tage points. Metascientifically, it offers a new scientific world
> view, replacing the previous one of mechanism with that of
> organized complexity. . . . It may be considered to serve as a
> science of systems or as a system of systems, thereby providing
> the framework for relating otherwise overwhelming collections
> of isolated facts and theories. Thus many see the usefulness of
> general systems theory in terms of its bridging functions, in
> which its cross-disciplinary language, its strongly convergent
> trends, and its emphasis on isomorphism play large roles. In
> these ways it offers potential for lessening the gap between the
> biological and the mental, the social and the cultural, the spe-
> cialist and the generalist, and between theory and practice. In its
> open, organismic and evolutionary qualities it provides a most
> congenial framework within which to consider problems of
> growth and change. (p. xx)

This offered a new context within which to work on the larger problems of the 20th century. Its impact on the tradi-tional social service and mental health structures was impor-tant since it presented a different way of viewing, for example, the problems of poverty, racism and urban decay. With the recognition that traditional treatment methods were not effec-tive in dealing with the problems posed by those urban pres-sures that were an integral part of the lives of the clients who came to these facilities, helping methods had to be developed to deal with those factors that so affected the quality of family life. Agencies firmly rooted in the concepts of family therapy had in a sense moved beyond the individual to a system more encompassing, but the further enlarging effect of systems the-ory with its fluid and integrative concepts would contribute to the development of a treatment method more genuinely re-sponsive to the client population. Edgar H. Auerswald (1969), the Director of the Family Mental Health Clinic at Jewish

Family Service at this time and a proponent of the ecological systems approach, stated,

> The "systems" approach, on the other hand, changes the vantage point of the data collector. It focuses precisely on the interfaces and communication processes taking place there. It begins with an analysis of the structure of the field, using the common structural and operational properties of systems as criteria for identifying the systems and subsystems within it. And by tracing the communications within and between systems, it insists that the structure, sources, pathways, repositary sites, and integrative functions of messages in addition to their content become clear. In my opinion, this, plus the holistic, non-exclusive nature of the approach, minimizes the dangers of excessive selectivity in the collection of data and allows for much more clarity in the contextual contributions to its analysis. And the steps which follow including prescriptions and planning of strategies and techniques, gain in clarity and are more likely to be rooted in concrete realities. (p. 375)

The 1960s helped us to recognize the need to be more a part of our clients' community life. Then and now, families who come to social service agencies have often been forced to relocate as a result of urban decay, wrenched away from where they have felt themselves to be rooted. Parents and children are too often faced with family breakdown as divorce has increased. As the economic hardships of escalating inflation and rising unemployment persist, more families have been and are faced with issues of poverty never before known. Suddenly public assistance and food stamps are no longer exclusively for "others." Urban centers like New York City have been ripped apart by issues of school decentralization and community control of neighborhood schools. Where previously there had been a sense of stability, the school has become for parents and children alike a place of potential unrest, uncertainty, and even violence. Systems theory offers a way of viewing the individual and family within this larger context. No longer is it necessary to separate them from the community and from the stresses and supports encountered daily. With the orientation of systems theory,

> such an emphasis makes it possible to determine with much more clarity in what life arenas the individual, the family, or a group of individuals needs assistance, and thus to combat more effectively the anomie and dehumanization characteristic of our age. (Auerswald, 1969, p. 377)

The hospital that offers our clients medical attention, the school that the children attend, the welfare investigator who reviews the family finances, the health system that approves or disapproves medical expenses, or the policeman who arrests the runaway teenager cannot be ignored as irrelevant to the family's problems. The recognition of these structures as systems with an internal life, as well as interrelationships with the family's operation, is essential in order to understand the multiple factors that contribute to change.

Traditional Intake Services

By reviewing the intake services offered by Jewish Family Service of New York City in the late 1960s the inherent problems in this system that were highlighted during this time can be pinpointed and the distance traveled in the development of a new service, Quick Response, made clearer. Since these practices and procedures are still used today by some social service and mental health facilities throughout the country, it is important to understand just why and where the changes were made.

TELEPHONE RECEPTION.   Neither an awareness of the client's crisis state nor a recognition of the increased anxiety that inevitably accompanies the initial request for help was sufficiently reflected in the design of the intake procedures.

The first telephone call was answered by a clerk-receptionist who took information from the client. The function of this clerk-receptionist was to listen to and record the client's problem as it was presented and to request important identifying data, so the client's initial experience with the agency consisted mostly of supplying information about himself or herself and the immediate situation. There was no immediate professional exchange in response to this presentation and the client then had to wait until a social worker returned the call. Although many agencies have a clerical worker handle the entire telephone reception, at Jewish Family Service professional intervention was considered helpful in conveying to the client that this call was a first step toward getting help. Even more important, though, was the professional's ability to pick up facets of a presentation not explicitly stated; to have the discipline to relate more to the client; and to provide direction, especially in a state of emergency when certain determinations and plans were needed immediately. Since the agency was also firmly rooted in the concepts of family therapy, this practice provided the reception social worker with an opportunity to encourage the client to engage other family members to attend the intake interview.

However, once the concepts of the client's crisis state and increased accessibility to intervention are taken into account, a further problem in the old, two-step process becomes apparent. Almost invariably difficulty was encountered when trying to return the applicant's call, resulting in further delays. To list but a few of the problems, many people call from their place of work and have limited time to use the phone, while others cannot be easily called back. Mothers are often out of the house doing errands, and finally, some people who do not have a phone will call from a friend's home. As the client experiences the time-lapse between this initial request for help and the actual opportunity to speak to a social worker, he or she is bound to feel more put off and unheard. Needless to say, much professional time is also wasted when return calls result in no answer. The longer it takes for a client to connect on the phone with the professional person who is there to hear him, the more is lost from both a therapeutic and economic point of view. While every agency has a right and even a responsibility to define when, how, and to whom it can be helpful based on a delineation of the service provided, once the crisis nature of the request for help is understood and the context of a systems framework developed, the difficulties of distinguishing over the telephone which clients can appropriately be helped by the agency's service and which cannot becomes more apparent. Requests for help are made in a variety of ways: the client's manner can be direct, coherent, and cooperative, or it can be unclear, off the point, and even disagreeable. The presented problem may or may not be the real concern. Many clients begin with a proposed solution to their difficulty that is actually a cover for the real problem. However, at the point of the initial telephone call the client is often very involved in his or her presentation; thus attempts to differentiate appropriate from inappropriate requests at this point may screen out many clients who could otherwise be helped during an appointment. For example, a client telephoned the agency requesting the recommendation of a good kosher caterer for her son's Bar Mitzvah. If the worker had responded to this request with either the name of a caterer or a statement that the agency did not provide this service, she would never have learned about the real problem, the woman's emotional struggle with her husband over the Bar Mitzvah.

A successful referral often requires the time and skill of a full interview to afford an understanding of the real nature of the crisis, to determine appropriate resources for assistance, and to help the client accept the recommendation. Even when the client would be best helped elsewhere with that part of the problem stated on the phone, other unrevealed aspects of the problem may well be something with which the agency can and should help. The chances are better that a more complete picture of the problem will emerge during an in-person interview than on the telephone.

Mrs. Berger telephoned the agency to request financial assistance because money had become just too tight to manage the support of her three children. While, in fact, the services of the local Department of Public Assistance were needed, many of her feelings of humiliation and ambivalence about this were not revealed until the reception interview. Although she believed this step to be inevitable, she was having difficulty facing it and a telephone referral to the local office of the Department of Public Assistance would not have been in and of itself a constructive intervention. During the interview Mrs. Berger also indicated that her current financial bind resulted from her father's recent death. Having been dependent on him for additional support, the loss was both a financial and an emotional one.

INTAKE APPOINTMENT AND WAITING LIST.   With this old system the intake appointment at Jewish Family Service was often with someone other than the telephone-reception worker. Procedurally, the first available time was pulled from a schedule of appointments previously set aside by designated workers and could range from 1 to 4 weeks after the reception call. Two intake appointments were sometimes needed to involve the whole family in the process of defining the problem and deciding about ongoing treatment. While family involvement was not a criterion for treatment, the agency orientation placed strong emphasis upon early participation of as many family members as possible. Although in some instances the intake appointment provided a complete service, there was a tendency to focus on the problem as having extended over a longer period of time and the current expression as only a starting point. In fact, the very term intake or reception implies an expectation of more to come and usually the recommendation was for continued treatment.

In most instances, after the intake appointment(s) the clients were transferred to a waiting list for continued service. Just as with telephone reception, there was again separation and discontinuity from a social worker (a third person if we count the clerk-receptionist), along with a wait for continued service and the introduction of another professional person. By this time, the client had made two beginnings and two endings. If for either emotional or concrete reasons the client could not wait for service, his or her place on the waiting list might be pushed forward, but usually he or she had to wait, go elsewhere, or try again to solve his or her own problems. All this waiting, all this stopping and starting was necessitated by an intake service that for all practical purposes screened clients for a more prolonged, open-ended treatment. The operational system and the philosophical orientation depend upon and reinforce each other.

Inevitably the client who had the ability, both situational and emotional, to delay a more immediate solution to the problem stood a far better chance of progressing past the intake procedures to continued service. This process worked against those clients who had a concrete problem whose solution could not be postponed, who were in such emotional distress that they psychologically could not wait, or whose social orientation was more present and less future oriented. Therefore, built into the reception process was the likelihood that more middle-class than lower-class clients would receive both an intake appointment and ongoing service since the lower class family is more often beset with pressing concrete problems that cannot wait for solution and more often has a social orientation that has less faith in the usefulness of waiting. As Helen Harris Perlman (1965) notes,

> the person of low socioeconomic status (when this is combined with limited education and narrow, hand-to-mouth existence) is not likely to have waiting capacity, hopefulness, or belief in help that he cannot see, smell, or take hold of . . . . when this nurture is withdrawn and he is told to hold his needfulness until the agency can find time to help him, the experience becomes just one more frustration. (p. 198)

However, even the middle-class oriented client who made it through this process was affected by delays and separations in the wait for service.

Of greatest concern even then was the waiting list that periodically accumulated with this intake system. Clients sometimes waited as long as 6 months, clearly too long for those whom the agency had determined were in need of service. In truth, the waiting list then became a phantom one and the chance to be helpful was often lost since many clients were no longer interested when offered service; they had either gone elsewhere for help or said the problem had been solved. Since a client's situation does not remain static and must be coped with in some way, even those who were ready to begin continued service when time was available were in a different position and had really to start over.

Problems for the agency as well as pitfalls for the client were inherent in this system. Failure to continue after being on the waiting list meant a good deal of professional effort had been lost and much time transferring a case to the waiting list was wasted. Besides the time spent with the client, the case record had been dictated, a consultation had sometimes been held, a supervisor had read the record, the waiting-list supervisor had reviewed it, and the newly assigned worker had spent time reading and reviewing the case, and contacting the client. In addition to professional time, clerical time is also amassed in typing and processing these records (Perlman, 1965). With the publication in 1962 of D. F. Beck's *Patterns in Use of Family Agency Service,* it became clear that the problems and concerns of Jewish Family Service in respect to these issues were not unique. The FSAA study reported that half of the clients studied who stayed on a waiting list for service for 9 weeks or more did not return. Consistent with JFS's own findings was the FSAA report that 90% of an agency's casework time was spent with 10% of the client population (Beck, 1962). Conclusively, too many clients who requested help were lost in the intake and waiting process and thus screened out of the agency's service. Certainly this alone gave significant cause for a critical evaluation of this process.

Precursors of Change

It is interesting to look back at the seeds of change, which were, with hindsight, so evident well before the actual birth of something new. Agencies, like individuals, have their own way of testing the waters before actually jumping in. In 1969, approximately a year before the inception of the Quick Response Service, a number of special projects were already in operation that began to test out these new theories. One such project, funded in part by federal funds, was called the *West Side Crisis Unit.* Its population was drawn from a geographically defined area and its purpose was to help people in crisis over a brief period of time, mainly through use of the ecological systems approach. Most clients walked into the storefront office from the street and service began at the moment of entry. Traditional intake methods and screening procedures were not practiced and this service operated in marked contrast to what was being offered in the main agency offices. Another pilot project, the *Village Project,* was a neighborhood-based crisis intervention service set up in a part of New York City heavily populated by runaway adolescents from all over the Northeast. Newer forms of supervision were tried in both projects; there was a move away from the more traditional and hierarchical structure of supervision to group supervision and peer-oriented consultation. Still another special project, *Project Enable,* was aimed exclusively at ghetto areas in an attempt to reach out to and involve persons from poverty areas not usually reached by the agency. Usual methods of office-bound treatment were replaced by field visits and community involvement. This reaffirmed the need for financial assistance in the repertoire of services offered by an agency if a more responsive and relevant service was to be devised.

Principles of Quick Response

By 1970, Quick Response was established to replace the existing intake service and provide immediate ongoing treatment to all clients who called or walked into the agency for help. Quick Response is a time-limited treatment that utilizes principles of crisis intervention and systems theory and has a firm rooting in family therapy. The client is understood to be requesting help at a point of crisis when the usual coping mechanisms have failed to work. Treatment begins immediately at the point of application and the worker who first has contact with the client continues until completion of service. Since the crisis results from some upset in the client's or family's homeostasis with which they cannot cope, the request for help is viewed as an attempt to forestall a threatened breakdown. The client's state of crisis is brought on by one or more of the following factors: (1) an internal conflict with which he or she cannot cope; (2) disequilibrium within the family system; (3) adverse or unmanageable influences within the larger environmental system. Since crises are understood to have a self-limiting time span of roughly 6 weeks (Caplan, 1964, p. 73; Golan, 1978, p. 9; Rapoport, 1965, p. 26), treatment is paced to coincide with this cycle and has a time-limited structure of up to six sessions. This allows for a concentrated piece of work on changes that are realistic and related to the client's/family's current crisis. Since time is conceived of dynamically, the arrangement of how long and how often the client is to be seen must flow in a nonstatic way from his or her particular situation. The overall limit of up to six sessions builds into the process the structure of a beginning, middle, and end phase of treatment.

Since the client all too often comes with not only his or her own individual problem but also as a spokesperson for a larger family concern, the worker moves quickly into the family system in order to be effective in helping them cope with the crisis within a limited period of time. The confines of the problem must often be expanded to include other systems within the client's environment to sufficiently understand the pressures that are creating or maintaining the problem. Consequently, it is sometimes necessary to leave the office and to meet, explore, and work with the client within the natural setting of the crisis. Thus the Quick Response worker has to be sufficiently sensitive to know when to enter the larger ecological system, rather than always to expect the family to reveal the whole of the situation within the artificial boundaries of the office.

The elements contributing to the crisis must be understood and better adaptive or coping mechanisms developed in order to help re-establish a state of homeostasis. Since a lack of resolution was what created the crisis, the client will hopefully leave treatment with better adaptive resources and increased ego strengths. The means of meeting the crisis should result in a family system more beneficial to the individual family members and/or help to create a better balance within the larger ecological system.

Chapter 2

BEGINNING PHASE
OF TREATMENT

The application of a Quick Response service to the setting of
a family agency is best understood when there is an appreciation of the full scope of human problems that come under its
auspices. Requests for help come from individuals, couples,
families, and intergenerational units. Clients live alone, with
relatives, with friends, or as part of a community group. Problems involve emotional concerns and concrete needs. People
call at the recommendation of friends, relatives, religious lead-
ers, another community agency, or an advertisement. The
client's psychiatric diagnoses can range from situational difficulty to decompensating schizophrenia. Universal issues such
as independence and dependence, separation and loss, and
questions of self-esteem are always involved. To consider just a
few examples: A wife calls about problems with her husband
and requests marital counseling; a mother is concerned about a
problem her child is having in school and wants some advice;
an adult son needs help with an aging parent; an adolescent is
having difficulties socializing; a family is unable to cope with

the death of a family member; divorce leaves the children in a family inordinately anxious, depressed, or rebellious. Financial problems result from the loss of a job, changes in welfare regulations, and housing difficulties. Illness causes turmoil of a concrete and emotional nature and community facilities such as day care, homemaking, and escort services may be needed. Aging parents may suddenly panic over plans for an increasingly violent and psychotic son who has for many years remained in his room. Help is needed to apply for medicaid, food stamps, or pension benefits. The list is endless, but it is important to understand the enormous range of people, problems, and situations that a family service agency must be prepared to meet when serving the needs of its community. Most applications start with the client's telephone call to the agency and the Quick Response service begins there.

As previously stated, the client calls the agency in a state of crisis resulting from an inability to cope with a problem that threatens his or her more balanced state. The resulting distress and anxiety may be experienced and handled in innumerable ways, but the person telephones the agency with hope for a solution and relief from his or her discomfort. Crisis theory emphasizes the heightened opportunity for impact at this point due to this increased urgency and receptivity. Thus an essential ingredient of Quick Response is that the worker take this telephone call immediately, avoiding the clerical questions and forms that so often create delay in initiating the process.

TELEPHONE RECEPTION

Purpose and Objectives

During this first telephone conversation, both parties are at a disadvantage because they do not know each other and lack the benefit of a face-to-face meeting. Since the telephone connection is so easily severed, a feeling of tentativeness is present. Because of their anxiety about requesting help, clients often begin speaking in a rush without even recognizing that a second person is on the telephone. The Quick Response worker must first make some connection with the client: usually an offer of one's name and some acknowledgement of availability helps the client to know the worker is there and wants to listen. Although most clients begin by spontaneously telling why they have called, they vary in how much or little they are willing to reveal over the phone and deal in different ways with their anxiety about calling. Some are passive and dependent, eager to tell their story, and wait for direction; others are reticent and suspicious, inclined toward distance and opposition if the worker reponds with much guidance. These nuances of behavior make telephone reception difficult, so it helps to understand that the client is acting defensively.

It is usually possible during the opening dialogue to discern many of the basic facts about the client's situation, rather than requiring responses to an agency questionnaire. Attempts to explore or probe beyond making a connection and getting some sketchy view of the problem are usually counterindicated at this stage unless the possibility of serious destructive behavior is indicated. In general, however, comments and reflections on the client's emotional state are best reserved for when the client and worker actually meet.

Although difficulties can result when there is too much probing, other problems may occur if there is too little. When the client begins by suggesting a solution to his problem rather than presenting the problem, it is likely to be one that either has not worked or cannot. If the worker fails to understand the nonproductive situation unwittingly being created and responds negatively to the suggestion, premature closing off can result. A better intervention is to request more information about the problem instead of immediately responding with an answer. Examples of this situation are numerous: a client calls to request money, legal services, an apartment, or that a child be taken to court. All of these may or may not be valid questions for exploration, but unless the discussion is opened up to allow for entry, the first step of making a connection with the client will never occur.

Even on the telephone the client feels some ambivalence and resistance to the exposure involved. If these feelings are sufficiently in check to allow movement in a constructive and unobstructed direction, then there is no reason to interfere. If, however, the client is obviously in need of help but is hampered by anxieties, then intervention is needed to assist her or him in moving ahead. Often clients become frightened when they do not feel that their suggested solution to the problem has been sufficiently recognized. The worker needs to understand this and to gauge his or her response in such a way that the exchange can progress. Naturally this task is difficult because what is needed by one client is not necessarily the same as what is needed by another.

Simply stated, the objectives of the first telephone conversation are to make an initial connection with the client, to discern some general idea as to the nature of the problem, and, in most instances, to move toward an appointment. In truth, however, these tasks require skill and discipline to accomplish.

Setting of First Appointment

TIME.   To be most responsive to the client's request for help, the Quick Response worker is freed from the traditional scheduling constraints that have in the past limited her or his ability to best meet the needs of a full range of clients who telephone an agency for help. If an appointment has to fit into an already fixed schedule, usually limited to the locale of the office, more responsive alternatives are greatly curtailed. Therefore, Quick Response allows a more flexible use of time in a way that is more related to individual needs. The client can be seen right away, scheduled for a few days later, or arrangements made with the client for a return call. The worker may spend 15 minutes or 5 hours with the client. The system allows time to be used dynamically in the crisis, rather than expecting the client to fit into a structure that is arbitrary and fixed.

The flexible use of time can seem at first staggering for those of us who have been schooled in more structured ways. Perhaps a few examples will prove helpful.

Mrs. Annenberg telephoned the agency sounding quite upset; her voice quavered and she talked between sobs. It was difficult to understand the problem and the worker gently suggested to Mrs. A. that perhaps she could come to the office right away so they could sit and talk together. When given this possibility, Mrs. A. calmed down enough to discuss directions to the office, and she arrived within the hour.

Mrs. Ross was in town only briefly for her sister's funeral and called to request help with planning for her adult mentally retarded nephew. The Quick Response worker's availability to meet with the nephew and her that day aided in involving a family network in planning for this man that may not have otherwise been possible.

John, age 15, called and said that he was considering running away from home. The worker recognized that because of the acting-out defenses so frequently in play during adolescence, he needed to be seen right away. Otherwise, John's conflict would likely be temporarily discharged through action and any appointment set up for a later time not kept.

Mrs. J. called to request an appointment because of a problem she was having with her husband and appropriately preferred to wait a few days so they could come together for a scheduled evening appointment.

Mrs. S. wanted help with a problem that her son was having in school and agreed it would be better to come the following evening with the whole family.

Many times a scheduled appointment of an hour's length is needed, while in other instances the client should be seen immediately just for 15 minutes to make contact and plan an appointment that will involve others. The possibilities are innumerable and the flexible use of time at the beginning can make a crucial difference as to how the practitioner helps the client to meet the crisis.

PLACE.   Responsiveness to client need involves flexibility about where to see the client as well as when; therefore, the Quick Response worker uses his or her own mobility as an option. The client can be seen at home or at some other place in his ecological system, as well as in the office. While often the neutrality, privacy, and structure of an office visit is the most helpful, this is not universally so and the demands of the situation may require a field visit. Homebound clients, for example, may because of their physical and/or emotional makeup not be able to travel to the office. Others may be under so many pressures that the added pressure of getting to the office is too much. For example, a woman who is distraught and overwhelmed after having recently lost her husband, and who is now the sole support for her seven children, could not be expected to travel to the office with seven children; yet to have suggested she come alone would have extremely limited the worker's view of her situation. Many agencies have traditionally provided a home visit in such instances, but not very soon after the initial application.

FAMILY INVOLVEMENT.   Although family therapy is by now a generally accepted form of psychotherapy, it is by no means the only treatment modality. However, family therapy is integral to the principles and practice of Quick Response, and is consistent with those elements of crisis and systems theory discussed throughout this presentation. To be helpful to a person or persons quickly at the crucial point of crisis and to do this within a time-limited period necessitate entering into the family system within which the crisis is running its course. Thus the person telephoning often expresses not only personal concern but has the dual function of acting as a family spokesperson. The homeostatic balance of the family system has been thrown off kilter and the family is having difficulty righting it.

If it is a more individual concern the supportive or destructive influences of other family members must be taken into consideration. Therefore, the Quick Response worker may suggest during the telephone reception that other family members come with the caller for the first appointment. Often clients themselves recognize the problem as involving others and all that is needed is confirmation of the importance of their participation. At other times the suggestion that a sibling, for example, be included in the first appointment is helpful. While some agencies indicate they have difficulties in involving the father in treatment, this problem is usually eliminated when evening hours are available and the importance of his participation is conveyed. Any appointment that interferes with the breadwinner's work will be experienced as difficult to arrange; it does not necessarily reflect the person's view of himself or herself in the problem, nor a lack of desire to be part of the solution.

On the other hand there are people who when they call are ready to be seen and need an appointment by themselves. This includes isolated and alone people in the community who are, for all practical purposes, without family or even friends. Additionally, a person may telephone about a problem that concerns others but may not want to include them or believes the other person(s) will not participate. It is important to begin with this person and not to attempt at that moment to understand the reasons behind his or her position. Trying to push in one direction or the other on the telephone is counterindicated, since the meaning of the position is unclear, and therefore so is the appropriate action. This can be better determined during an in-person interview.

SYSTEMS ACTIVITY.   Many clients request help from a social service agency because an agent in their community has suggested they seek help, not because they view the situation as necessitating it. At times this referral is made constructively and at other times with the threat of unpleasant consequences if the person does not comply. Therefore, the client may call with mixed feelings about whether he or the community agent is the one with the problem. Examples of school, hospital, welfare department, and vocational resource referrals come to mind. Often really "beginning where the client is" requires a field visit to the referring resource for a meeting with both the prospective clients and the referring person. To gain a more comprehensive and accurate picture of the client's crisis, the Quick Response worker must understand the system in operation.

Mrs. Anderson called the agency stating that she had been directed by the principal of her son's school to set up an appointment immediately or else he would be expelled. Inevitably this kind of beginning leads to distortions about the agency's role and other possible areas of misunderstanding. To begin working with this family without instituting some clarifying intervention would invariably lead to a muddle that could take much time and effort to straighten out. Meanwhile weeks would transpire and the crisis that prompted Mrs. A. to call would go underground. Consequently, a three-way meeting at the school with the Anderson family, the school representatives, and the worker was arranged in order to clarify the issues from the beginning.

Ray Dobbs, a young man in his early 20s, indicated when he called for an appointment that the medical examiner at his place of employment had said he could not return to work until he began a counseling program. Here again, a meeting with the prospective client, the medical examiner, and the Quick Response worker helped clarify issues and define areas of concern, and differentiated functions that could never be accomplished without a field visit to investigate this pertinent part of the client's ecological system. Only then could the crisis be clarified and decisions made regarding how to be helpful.

Each situation is unique, however, and therefore necessitates its own response. While Quick Response allows flexibility of time and mobility, the worker must not blindly go and do. Professional discipline necessitates listening and discerning. Many a client during this initial telephone call will define the problem as not his or her own but that of someone else, and will request a home visit for this other person, leaving himself or herself out or only marginally involved. Rather than agreeing, a suggestion that the person who calls come either alone or along with the person with whom he or she is concerned may be in order.

Mr. J. called about his 25-year-old son, Phillip, who had been secluded in his bedroom for 6 months. Recently his temper tantrums at night had increased and the father wanted someone to take his son to a hospital. Although Mr. J.'s request that the agency take over and allow him to back out might become necessary at some point, the first step was to meet Mr. and Mrs. J. in the office and to begin with them.

The person who telephones requesting help has some part to play in the situation and cannot be left out. Although the caller may be only a link to the person who will become a client, she or he is yet a link not to be overlooked.

Mrs. Loren telephoned to request help for her niece, who had two young children and was having so much difficulty coping with them she had spoken to her aunt about placement. The aunt requested that the worker telephone the niece to offer help. The worker instead suggested that an appointment time convenient for Mrs. Loren be set up so that she could accompany her niece and the children. After reassurance that this would probably be only for the initial appointment, Mrs. Loren agreed even though it meant a 2-hour automobile trip for her. Subsequently, the worker discovered that two previous appointments made for the niece alone had not been kept. When they all came for the appointment, Mrs. Loren's assistance was crucial in helping her niece convey just how desperate she felt. Without the aunt's participation, treatment would probably never have begun.

Certain unique characteristics thus constitute a Quick Response service from the very beginning. First, since both immediacy and continuity of service are essential, a professional person takes the initial telephone call and is available as soon as necessary to see and continue with the client. Second, flexibility as to the time allotted and the place designated for beginning flows in a nonstatic way from the particular needs of the situation. These responses to the client upon the first telephone contact helps to create a positive and strong bond between the client and the worker. The quickness and flexibility with which help is offered stimulate positive transferential feelings; the strength of this can contribute to treatment beginning in a more trusting and constructive atmosphere.

Even the attempts to keep exploration and probing to a minimum during the telephone reception have opened up many more ways of being responsive to a client. In some ways these attempts make the task more difficult and in other ways easier. No longer limited to a confined and rigid set of alternatives, the structure that may have previously seemed at least superficially comforting has now been eliminated and we are left having to "listen to" what the client is saying, and to respond accordingly. Although this may appear to create an additional demand on the worker, when these responses are truly geared to the client's need and unique circumstances, a first appointment is easier to arrange and is more likely to be kept.

Walk-ins

Certain clients walk into an agency without calling for an appointment and want help right away. Any number of explanations for such behavior are possible, but the only result of refusing to see the person is the loss of the opportunity to understand why. Some clients are too disorganized and confused in their functioning to consider planning ahead. Others are not yet ready to ask directly for help and "just stop by on their lunch hour for a card." Some are in such emotional distress they have to be seen immediately and experience the situation as a state of emergency. No diagnostic category or situational picture can be drawn a priori about the walk-in situation. However, all that has been discussed about crisis theory and the importance of availability applies to the walk-in as well as to the client who telephones.

BEGINNING IN-PERSON CONTACT

Certain principles of a first appointment (walk-in or planned) crucial to beginning with any client, whether in Quick Response or some other mode of treatment, are worth reviewing. An appreciation of the fact that any client has probably been under considerable duress from her or his own internal conflict, familial disharmony, or environmental threat helps to underscore the importance of a neutral, benign, and receptive atmosphere. The client/family needs to perceive the worker as a person who will not judge and retaliate in any of the ways so recently experienced. Many people come for help because of problems with others in their social environment. A certain amount of projection is usually operative, families are involved in some scapegoating and collusiveness, and blame and anger may have reached a destructive level. In this climate it is important not to join or to deny but rather to allow an environment to develop in which some understanding can be gained. Even the client who comes with the sole expectation that the other person will be gotten off his back has been under pressure. His conception of the problem and hoped-for solution are not a measure of how it felt to live with the crisis.

It is impossible to enumerate here all the professional skills involved, but professionals must be able to provide the client with assistance in explaining what has brought him or her for help and what attempts have been made thus far to cope with the crisis. Generalities, abstractions, accusations, and the presentation of feelings as if they were facts are all common occurrences. The real work begins with helping the client(s) present a more specific and complete picture. Events must be described in more behavioral terms; feelings thus emerge from this, rather than floating freely. Nonverbal clues are vital to understanding the individual and the dynamics of a family system; how a person is dressed, where everyone sits, how facial expressions coincide with what is being said, where other family members look when another is speaking, who fails to speak. During this beginning period of exploration and investigation, covert views of problem and solution need to surface. Family members will each see the problem differently and will even disagree with another's statement about it. In actuality there may be a good deal of reluctance and even suspicion about the appointment. This often is true when a family member has been pushed into coming or when some community authority with real or fantasized power has pressured them. Only by enabling each person to speak as honestly and as openly as possible will the problem be understood in a substantial way and the client's real engagement in a treatment process evolve.

When clients first come for help their usual coping mechanisms have been largely ineffective in dealing with the crisis at hand. More primitive defense mechanisms may be employed to prevent anxiety-producing material from surfacing. Client(s) may use displacement, projection, or denial to avoid the real source of anxiety. At times the defenses are only thinly disguising the problematic conflict and the client partially points the way. As one family member moves in one direction, another indicates a different direction. Sometimes the most fruitful area for exploration is the one nobody wants to discuss. Valuable information can be gained in the beginning by observing the modes of interaction, affectual states, and defense mechanisms. Basic elements of family structure such as lines of authority, collusive alliances, competitive relationships, and scapegoating maneuvers can be observed. Preliminary diagnostic material such as the appropriateness of the client's behavior, mood in relation to speech content, presence of any thought disorders, and other such phenomena need to be evaluated.

This brief review serves to emphasize that regardless of

the treatment modality, certain principles of evaluation and engagement must be practiced as a given part of any beginning process. If these are skipped over or rushed through neither Quick Response nor any other treatment process will work as it should.

The Precipitating Crisis

The work of Quick Response focuses on the crisis that has caused the current disequilibrium in the individual/ family system and the emphasis of work is on the here and now. Uncovering, defining, and understanding the precipitating crisis is a complicated and multifaceted process and it is here that the work begins when client(s) and worker first meet. Hoffman and Remmel (1975) offer a comprehensive and succinct explanation of the development of a crisis.

> The core conflict is ever-present, but dormant. An emotional hazard or catalyst such as menopause or a loss of a relationship disturbs the dormant conflict, but does not arouse it fully. The conflict is in a fitful state—neither asleep nor awake. However, the potential for eruption is increased because of the occurrence of the emotional hazard. If the person is able to handle the emotional hazard by using his customary coping mechanisms . . . the emotional hazard will not be converted into a crisis situation. If, however, the person is not able to cope with the emotional hazard, he will experience some precipitating event which, along with the special meaning this event has for him (precipitant), will fully arouse the dormant conflict and cause eruption (crisis, state of disequilibrium). (p. 260)

While Hoffman and Remmel have discussed this development in terms of an individual, the description applies also to the family system; a normally dormant family conflict is partially aroused by an emotional hazard that, if not dealt with by the family's usual coping devices, will lead to a precipitating event that will catapult the whole family into crisis. A similar chain of events can occur among an individual/family and elements of their ecological system to create the crisis.

During the first Quick Response appointment, focus should be on moving from the client's presented problem to determining the precipitating event and precipitant that have led to the present crisis. In order to accomplish this, a skillful and directed exploration is necessary, including relevant questions about the client's current life, historical information that provides a more rounded picture of the situation, reflections about contradictory elements in the client's presentation, inquiries as to relationships with significant others, and, naturally, a more thorough investigation of the material presented. However, caution must be exercised not to be enticed into other nonrelated problematic areas; only by staying with the current crisis can treatment be effective and time-limited.

Mrs. Jacobs telephoned the agency requesting help in deciding if her daughter's analyst was qualified. In addition, she was feeling depressed recently and, although she had been on a diet and lost 45 pounds, she was now afraid of gaining them back. Mrs. J. was offered an appointment and seen 2 days later. She was a tall, brunette woman, neatly dressed and somewhat overweight. She had been divorced many years previously, lived by herself, and had worked regularly for a long time as a restaurant cashier. Her daughter Joan, 30, was married and had not lived with her for 7 years. Her other daughter Angel, 25, had lived on her own since a psychiatric hospitalization 3 years previously.

Mrs. J. was an anxious woman who worked overtime to anticipate problems, worry about their solution, and ruminate as to how things could have been different. Her major defense was obsessive-compulsive, her relationships were marginal and tangential, and her superego operated intensively to keep her impulses in check. Mrs. J. began with several concerns, unspecific to the here and now; she was worried about others rejecting her, about gaining weight, and about feeling unattractive. Attempts were made to engage the worker in negative judgments about her and about the hopelessness of her situation. When encouraged to describe her present life, Mrs. J. emphasized the importance of her relationship with a boyfriend, Johnny. Although he was married and limited in his availability, their regular and reliable dates were important to her. She enjoyed the predominantly sexual contact without being frightened of being overwhelmed by more. Although Mrs. J. conveyed this general picture of her situation, the worker had to help her be more specific about the present circumstances that were creating her distress. Interestingly (and not unusual), Mrs. J. never mentioned the concern about her daughter's analyst to which she had alluded on the phone. When asked about it, Mrs. J. revealed that Angel had recently asked if she could move back home and Mrs. J. was in a conflict about what to do. She wanted to say no; clearly she did not want Angel home for a number of reasons, but especially because she did not want to have to manage her sexual activities with her daughter in the apartment. However, her fears and distortions about what her saying no to Angel would mean to both of them created a conflict that was intense and difficult for Mrs. J. to resolve.

In Mrs. J.'s ruminations about this she had mentioned it to Johnny. What had led Mrs. J. to telephone the agency was that Johnny had not shown up for the date scheduled after this discussion. Whether the reason for this had anything to do with their talk did not really matter because in Mrs. J.'s mind she was already being deprived of her sexual outlet after merely mentioning the possibility of allowing Angel back. The precipitating event in this instance was Johnny's breaking the date. The precipitant was that this reinforced her fears that to allow her daughter back home was, indeed, going to result in some loss for her and a reinstatement of the deprivation she experienced when a closer mother-daughter relationship had existed. The emotional hazard of her daughter possibly living with her again had reactivated conflictual material as to their relationship. As Mrs. J. spoke about this, it became clear that it was Angel's hospitalization and subsequent treatment that had enabled them to break the symbiotic cycle of merging, incorporation, and destructive rejection that had been present. Mrs. J. experienced saying no to Angel (which would have caused a realistic and appropriate separation) as an act of anger and rejection. Since she was a woman who held her sexual and aggressive impulses very tightly in check by fairly rigid defenses, the present pressure from both the heightened sexual and destructive forces were too much for her.

While it is possible in a first appointment to understand the precipitating event, the precipitant, and the emotional hazard, and even point to the core conflict, the worker and the client do not move at the same rate and do not understand this material in the same terms. This relates more to how the client is engaged and the extent of the engagement. Before turning to a discussion of this, however, some further examples of how to determine the precipitating event and precipitant are needed.

Mr. Evans, a school guidance counselor, telephoned the agency to refer Mrs. Rosenthal and her 9-year-old daughter, Evelyn, for help. Mrs. R. took the phone and explained that her daughter constantly cried and panicked whenever Mrs. R. did not feel well. Evelyn had trouble eating and sleeping and she objected to her mother's dating. Mrs. R. added as an aside that her husband had died 6 months previously. Although two other children were in the family, Sara, 21, and Henry, 11, Mrs. R. was hesitant to include them in an appointment, indicating the problem was mainly with Evelyn.

Mrs. R. and Evelyn came for the first appointment 2 days later. She was a bright, talkative, well-dressed woman who tried to appear in control but whose manner, nevertheless, was tense and pressured. Evelyn was much like her mother but quicker to show a vulnerable and softer side. Although Mrs. R. had indicated on the telephone that Evelyn's behavior was the problem, she began the first session explaining about her husband's illness and sudden death. Evelyn cried and spoke about how she missed her father. Although her mother had begun to cry and allude to feelings of loss and confusion, when Evelyn opened up Mrs. R. pulled herself together and explained that the problem centered around the children's reaction to her having recently met Mr. Abbott, and their dating and more recent discussions of marriage. Evelyn was most direct in her protestations about mother's going out. She would cry whenever he came over, wake up during the night when Mrs. R. was out, and lately stayed home from school with stomachaches. Mrs. R's decision to look for a job was too much for Evelyn. When Mrs. R. was to go for an interview, Evelyn became hysterical and only her mother's decision to stay home calmed her down. When Mrs. R. turned to Mr. Abbott for advice, he suggested she seek professional counseling. When the worker did not take sides, neither indicating Mrs. R. should give Mr. A. up nor marry him, that neither her children nor she were right, Mrs. R. was able to see the value of all the children attending the next appointment.

Just how much the family was struggling with the meaning of

Mr. R.'s death became clear during these two appointments. The currents were running strong both to deny and to allow the phenomenon of this loss to surface. Sara was the angriest and most belligerent of the children. While seemingly independent and working full-time, she was still supported by her mother but any overt expression of dependency and caring toward her was unacceptable to Sara. At the same time, Mrs. R. viewed and used Sara as the judge and jury who would always find her guilty. Henry was quieter and more involved in activities of different kinds. He played baseball, spent a lot of time out of the house, and tried with a moderate degree of success to stay out of other people's way.

Mrs. R. and Sara quickly began arguing at the beginning of the second session. Sara revealed that no one listened to Mrs. R. and that she never tried very hard to enforce her position. Sara felt her mother could do a better job but had stopped short of taking it on and abandoned her parental responsibility. Mrs. R. defensively explained how her husband had always been the disciplinarian in the family and she was ill-equipped to take his place. She quickly suggested a better solution would be to replace Mr. R. with a new Mr. R., such as Mr. Abbott. This clearly was the current bone of contention in the family. Whenever feelings about Mr. R.'s death began to surface, everyone quieted and began to cry. Inevitably, Mrs. R. got angry about something or at someone, indirectly leading all away from their grief. Most frequently she mentioned what a good replacement Mr. A. would be for her husband. The children understood not only that they should not mourn their father but that the only surviving parent was also moving away from them.

The precipitating event was twofold. During a recent discussion about the children's increasing pressure on her, Mr. A. had suggested they see each other less. Threatened with the loss of her husband-substitute, feelings about her husband's death that she had been working so hard to deny re-emerged. When she tried to escape by looking for a job, Evelyn made this avenue difficult to take and she was doubly pinned in. This meant (precipitant) that she might have to face her real loss and contemplate where this left her as a single parent. Her husband's death (emotional hazard) had reactivated old concerns about her ability to be independent and exercise authority over both herself and others. The children were more ready to deal with their reactions to their father's death but were being inhibited by mother's difficulties. Many unexpressed questions remained unanswered for them about who would be there to take his place.

Very often the precipitating event is sparked by an encounter with a community institution and is experienced by the client as an intrusive event. An inability to cope with the experience can facilitate a move toward professional help. Typical is the situation in which the school's contact with a parent about a child's behavior is coupled with an overt or covert threat of suspension. The impact of the event and the meaning it takes on for the parents cannot be quickly dismissed.

Mrs. Henderson, age 26, telephoned the agency for help at the suggestion of a co-worker. She had returned to work visibly shaken after a conference with her 6-year-old daughter Jo's principal and guidance counselor. When she shared her problem with a friend, the friend suggested Mrs. H. call for help.

While very sketchy as to what Jo's difficulties were at school, Mrs. H. was most concerned about the school's threat of suspension and their not-so-disguised criticism of her disciplinary methods. Both the principal and guidance counselor had told her that her practice of withholding privileges was an inadequate method of punishment. Although concerned about how to correct the situation, Mrs. H.'s presentation was weighted in terms of how she felt victimized in the encounter with these two professional women.

When the worker contacted the school authorities two very interesting elements emerged. The guidance counselor was indeed quite abrasive in her way of dealing with the worker, being curt and not very eager to allot much time to the discussion. She seemed to be a person who easily provokes annoyance and who necessitates a firm response. At the same time she presented a picture of Jo that substantiated the school's concern. She was always getting into physical fights with other children and frequently had temper tantrums when the teacher told her what to do.

The worker's attempts to understand the precipitating event and precipitant helped to reveal much about Mrs. H.'s conflictual state and how her daughter was being used in this struggle. Mrs. H.'s way of coping with her own aggressive impulses, experienced by her as fearful and unmanageable, was to interact with others in such a way that their behavior served as a controlling and inhibiting force for her. She presented herself as weak, uncertain, and easily intimidated by disagreement. Her ex-husband had been abusive to her; even now her in-laws set many of the rules. Historical information pointed to a similar negative complementarity between Mrs. H. and her mother. Mrs. H. experienced herself as often depressed, lonely, and, at times, just plain irritable. While some displacement of her anger onto Jo occurred, Mrs. H. more often had difficulty asserting herself constructively. The most pressing of her concerns was how to tell her in-laws that she wanted more privacy and did not want them visiting Jo without first calling. These issues of assertion and self-entitlement were touched on during the school conference and threatened to be unmanageable for her.

As the precipitating event was explored further, it became clear that Jo's behavior at school had become more destructively aggressive when the regular teacher, of whom she was very fond, took ill and had to be absent. Issues of separation and the accompanying fears and angers played heavily on this little girl's mind as well as on her mother's.

During the beginning phase the worker tries to move from the presented problem to an understanding of the precipitating event and the precipitant. At times some understanding about the emotional hazard and core conflict can be gained early. However, this beginning process must involve more than just information gathering. The process of engaging the client(s) is interwoven into this process and the extent to which the client is engaged in this movement will determine the course of treatment.

When the worker first meets the client, she or he must listen to and explore the client's presentation of the problem/situation in order to be able to assess the client's general psychological state and make a tentative diagnosis. While always subject to change, this diagnosis is used in determining how to engage the client. For example, the projections of a paranoid schizophrenic client require a different response than those of a passive-aggressive personality. Recognition of the difference between a leaderless family and a psychotic family is crucial to effective intervention. During this process, areas of resistance and defense mechanisms are noted. Usual coping mechanisms are strained because of this crisis and defenses can be loosened or rigidified in response. By actively testing these areas of resistance, it is possible to discover whether the defenses are more pliable than they at first appeared to be. For example, the strain of the present crisis may have loosened a client's passive stance so that he or she is now more conflicted about certain aspects of his or her behavior. Often during this period of exploration, clients provide information related to many problematic areas in their lives. The temptation to pick up on any number of these can be great, but recognition of this invitation as a defensive maneuver is crucial to a significant engagement of the client around the present crisis conflict. It is important to remember that this present difficulty was what motivated him or her to seek help.

The Quick Response worker must take a more active approach than in other forms of psychotherapy and in this respect is very much a family therapist. While every client needs to tell his own story, at his own pace, the practitioner must actively pursue areas alluded to but not readily entered; seek out historical material that could make present material more meaningful than is immediately apparent; give direction when everyone else is fearful; make connections that give meaning to what is being said; and confront issues and modes of behavior that others are reluctant to approach. At the same time, the capacity for an empathetic understanding is crucial in order both to uncover the crisis material and to engage the client in this process. Without this component the client cannot experience the support necessary to continue. Also important is that the Quick Response worker utilize and reinstate the cognitive functions of the ego which are so often impaired during the throes of a crisis. Client's fright and immobilization is lessened when certain phenomena are explained and her or his capacity to cooperate in the treatment work increases when a cognitive understanding is gained. Throughout this process, the worker's nonjudgemental attitude is conveyed, which helps decrease those self-punitive judgements that often interfere with the client's being able to work constructively.

Determining the Treatment Focus

Both the nature of the precipitating crisis and the client's engagement have to be considered in determining the treatment focus. At the conclusion of this beginning period the depth of understanding and extent of engagement can range on a continuum anywhere from the presented problem to the core conflict. The agents of the crisis involved in treatment may include the individual, family members, and environmental contributors. Since a crisis can be expressed in different areas of a person's life, treatment can be concentrated in one or more of these: the larger ecological system, the interactional life of the family, the individual's behavioral adaptation, and his or her internal psychic processes. The recognition that one area is no more or less valid than another is important to a proper consideration of the treatment focus.

In the Jacobs' case, previously discussed, the emotional hazard of Angel's possibly living with her mother again and how this had reactivated conflictual material as to their relationship were uncovered. The treatment focus was aimed at helping Mrs. J. with these issues and with the decision to be made. Movement from her diffuse presenting complaints to a recognition of what was precipitating the crisis enabled Mrs. J. to understand that her own thoughts and feelings about this decision needed sorting out and that this would be the treatment focus.

While our understanding of the crisis that brought the Rosenthal family for treatment was just as complete as in the Jacobs' case, the extent of the family's engagement was not. Although much was clear about how Mr. R.'s death had upset both the homeostasis of the family system and the intrapsychic balance of individual family members, the family's understanding did not evolve at the same pace as the worker's. All could recognize that Mr. R's death had left a gap in the family, that this was creating conflict, and that their ideas differed as how to resolve the situation. The children were more ready to face issues of mourning than Mrs. R., who remained more defended against her feelings and fears about this loss. However, she was able to recognize how Mr. A. was being used as an object of her own and the children's displacement and to focus more on the trouble the family was having reorganizing their interpersonal system. The extent to which each could focus on the individual significance of their loss varied and further recognition about this would be determined as treatment progressed. However, at the conclusion of this beginning phase, the extent of the clients' engagement determined that the treatment focus be predominantly on the level of the familial interaction.

The client's previous level of functioning and adaptive resources have to be considered when evaluating his engagement in this beginning process. A viable treatment focus can only be established in this context.

Mr. Abrams requested help from the agency when he was unable to pay his rent. He was an isolated 45-year-old man whose functioning had been marginal most of his life. He lived alone in a basement apartment and his only social contacts were neighborhood people who spoke to him mainly in passing. His primary relationship had been with his mother, who had died 15 years before. At that time he had been hospitalized briefly, but since then had made a marginal but stable adjustment, working steadily as a messenger for the same firm until 6 months previously. Diagnosed as a simple schizophrenic, his adjustment had been reasonably good before the present crisis and he had not requested help from a social service agency in the past 10 years.

During Mr. A's first appointment the worker was able to understand the important elements of his present crisis. The precipitating event had been Mr. A.'s landlord personally requesting the overdue rent when previous requests had been made in writing. The rent was, in fact, 4 weeks overdue since Mr. A. had been unable lately to find handyman jobs in the neighborhood. The precipitant was his experiencing the request as threatening because it stimulated not only his aggressive impulses but also abandonment fears that were very difficult for him to handle. The stage had been set a few months previously when Mr. A. lost his messenger job (emotional hazard). This confronted him with serious financial concerns and threatened to activate dormant conflicts around loss of the maternal object.

Although Mr. A. provided the material for the worker to piece together the significant element of this crisis, the presentation was detached and cognitively disorganized. Most concerned with how to pay the rent and worried that his everyday functioning was deteriorating, Mr. A. was developing a diffuse anxiety and seemed to be decompensating as a result of the present crisis. The worker shared this concern and concluded that the treatment needed to focus on helping Mr. A. deal with the landlord, pay the rent, and re-establish financial stability. Emphasis would be on tightening his weakening defenses and re-establishing the previous level of social functioning in the area of the precipitating event.

Setting the Treatment Focus into a Time-Limited Framework

Once the nature of the crisis is determined and the level of the client's engagement evaluated, the treatment focus needs to be set into a time-limited framework. As previously discussed, a crisis has a self-limiting time span of roughly 6 weeks and the period of upset can be divided into a beginning, middle, and end phase (Rapoport, 1965, p. 26). Quick Response has a time limit of up to six sessions, which creates a beginning, middle, and end phase to treatment. To determine a treatment focus that is both significant to the client and manageable within this time limit, it is important to pay attention to the present expression of the crisis. A treatment focus that is clear, defined, and limited in scope is easier to take hold of and work on successfully in up to six sessions. Before discussing just how the treatment focus and the time limit are introduced, further reflection about the ramifications of a time-limited treatment is needed.

RATIONALE FOR A TIME LIMIT.   The specific limitation of time built into Quick Response has as great an impact on the practitioner as the client. At first a desire to avoid and then even to resist this aspect of the treatment is typical. However, unless subjective as well as objective reactions are considered, the benefits to be gained from a time-limited psychotherapy will go unrealized. James Mann (1973), in *Time-Limited Psychotherapy,* notes, "One way of understanding the failure to give time central significance in short forms of psychotherapy lies in the will to deny the horror of time by the therapists themselves." (p. 10) He offers an important explanation as to why the limitation on time is so painful to recognize:

> Any psychotherapy which is limited in time brings fresh flame to the enduring presence in all persons of the conflict between timelessness, infinite time, immortality and the omnipotent fantasies of childhood on the one hand, and time, finite time, reality, and death on the other hand. The wishes of the unconscious are timeless and promptly run counter to an offer of help in which time is limited. Thus, any time-limited psychotherapy addresses itself both to child time and to adult time. At the least, this gives rise to powerful conflicting reactions, responses, and most of all, conflicting expectations. The greater the ambiguity as to the duration of treatment, the greater the influence of child time on unconscious wishes and expectations. The greater specificity of duration of treatment, the more rapidly and appropriately is child time confronted with reality and the work to be done. (pp. 10–11)

Every practitioner senses immediately that a definite plan from the beginning for treatment to last for a specific length of time challenges her or his own unconscious sense of timelessness and fantasies of omnipotence, in order to enable the ego functions associated with adult time to operate more effectively. With a heightened sense of the work to be done, he or she is reminded of the inevitability of separation and the end of treatment.

With an increased awareness of these dynamics, the worker can better appreciate the potential benefits of a time limit and there is less resistance to this form of psychotherapy. When the time limit is made explicit from the beginning it helps to check those unconscious infantile fantasies stimulated by a sense of timelessness in the client as well as the worker, and a more real sense of time helps to mobilize the client's ego strengths for the work at hand. The time limit provides treatment with a beginning, middle, and end, which more accurately reflects the structure of life. When coupled with a meaningful focus that is clear, limited, and manageable, the treatment is intensified and concentrated in a positive direction. Once the time limit has been introduced, attention must be paid to its impact but its effect cannot be measured solely by how the client responds at first. Since the meaning of time is not separate from such emotional issues as separation/loss, independence/dependence, adequacy/inadequacy, the client's reactions serve as a vehicle to express much about what brought her or him for help and provide a powerful tool with which to understand and help the client with the crisis.

PRESENTATION OF THE TREATMENT AGREEMENT.   The time limit should be introduced in conjunction with the treatment focus so that structure and substance are combined into a dynamic whole. Otherwise, the time limit is devoid of meaning until the client has some idea what direction the treatment work will take and for what purpose the time is to be used. To suggest a structure of up to six sessions serves no purpose if the client/family does not know whether they want to or need to return and thus reflects a premature introduction of the limitations on time. On the other hand, to define the treatment work regardless of the time limit fails to provide the client with a realistic structure. Combining the focus and time limit and presenting them in an understandable way is often experienced as an encouraging expression of confidence in success. To accomplish this, the treatment agreement (treatment focus and time limt) must be stated in a cognitively clear way so that the client can grasp it, and as emotionally related to his pain so that he feels empathetically understood. This challenges the client's ego strengths to work on the dilemma that is contributing to the crisis and conveys feelings of acceptance and support that help sustain him through the work. The proposal that a significant piece of work can be accomplished in the limited amount of time is experienced positively as long as the treatment focus is both central to the crisis and truly manageable within a six-session framework.

While on a conscious level the treatment agreement is seen as beneficial, on an unconscious level the client's more negative feelings about the constraints of time may be activated when a consensus on the treatment agreement is requested. Questions at this point about what will happen at the end of six sessions are disguised attempts to mediate the time limit and test out how firm a proposition this is. Typical at this point are questions about what will happen at the end of six sessions if the work has not been completed or the client feels more help is needed. It is essential that the worker hold firm to the proposed limitations on time and simultaneously convey his or her optimism that the work can be successfully accomplished within this period of time. To do anything less than this implies a willingness to compromise the time limit and not take it seriously. However, to dwell too long on this point only serves to bog down the treatment in material that will re-emerge later in a more meaningful way.

Since the time framework for a Quick Response case is up to six sessions, the amount of time offered at the point of the treatment agreement is the unused portion, usually five sessions. The beginning appointment(s) is part of the whole, not to be separated out and the process begun again. The option is presented as up to six sessions rather than a rigid six in order to emphasize that time is a dynamic phenomenon best utilized actively rather than as a stagnant point to be marked off on the calendar. All six sessions may be used but if the treatment goal is realized prior to this, treatment can be terminated.

In some instances the phenomenon of time can be made more explicit by specifying how long each appointment will last, how appointments are to be spaced, and even what the date of the last available session will be. However, this is often impossible because of a stronger need for flexibility on just these points. For example, the date and duration of a crucial meeting to be set up with a group in the client's ecological system cannot be projected at the beginning. The nature of a client's crisis may necessitate two appointments spaced closer together than the others, and inclusion of various family members at one session may lengthen the appointment time. Nevertheless, in order to convey in some way that treatment has a definite termination point, at the very least, the probable week of the sixth and therefore last available appointment can be noted.

The process involved in reaching a consensus on the treatment agreement (treatment focus and time limit) can be illustrated by returning to the Rosenthal family.

Toward the end of the second session, the first full family interview, it was possible to summarize for the family the problem they were experiencing that was causing the current disequilibrium. The worker stated simply that everyone was understandably full of their own reactions to Mr. R.'s death, but were unsure what to do with and how to express these reactions. As a family they had not as yet worked out a way of functioning without him. The struggle around Mr. Abbott had little to do with Mr. A. per se, but was really everyone's way of expressing their confusion about the loss of Mr. R. and who, if anyone, would take his place. With the quiet consensus that followed, the worker went on to suggest that they continue as a family to work out this difficulty and that the next four sessions would be available to them for this purpose. While all seemed relatively comfortable with the presentation of the treatment focus, there was varying reaction to the suggestion of a time limit.

Mrs. R. spoke first, quickly indicating that the proposal was all right with her but questioning whether the worker thought four sessions would allow sufficient time. Mrs. R.'s mixed reaction was understandable since she subconsciously sensed that the time limit in some way conflicted with her desire to avoid the issues of loss, separation, and parental responsibility. The question was also a test of the worker's willingness to allow for Mrs. R.'s dependency needs. The worker addressed herself to both issues by responding that she thought this would be sufficient time and emphasizing that they would be working together on this. In contrast, Sara quickly expressed her very definite opinion that four sessions would provide ample time for her. She undoubtedly used the time limit to support her need to avoid any overt expression of dependency. While not challenging this, the worker did respond to Sara's more genuine feelings of vulnerability by indicating that four sessions would allow everyone time to consider how difficult all of this had really been for them. Evelyn responded less to the time limit and more to what had been said about missing her father. Since Evelyn was clearly the family spokesperson about how vulnerable and adrift they really felt, the worker supported not only her feelings but also her courage in being so open with them, thus setting the tone for the work ahead. Henry, on the other hand, continued to be more reserved and his reaction had to be elicited. He was most concerned about missing the baseball game that was scheduled at the same time as the appointment, and this also symbolically referred to his worry about the loss in his life of the father whom he had experienced as nurturing and protective. Spontaneously Mrs. R. asked if the appointment day could be rearranged, for the first time in the interview moving to fill the parental role.

Once everyone had concurred on the treatment agreement, the appointment time, dates, and fee could be set. Special note was made of the date of the last appointment.

The next case summary will illustrate how the introduction of a time limit, when coupled with a treatment focus related to the client's crisis, can have a freeing and mobilizing effect on the family. The time limit is experienced as an expression of the worker's belief in the manageability of their crisis and in their ability to handle it successfully.

Mrs. Bennett called for help at the urging of a friend who was familiar with the Bennetts' present situation. Mr. and Mrs. B. had had many years of counseling in connection with various family problems. Their eldest daughter had died about a year previously from a long and disabling illness. The Bennetts viewed their many years of contact with mental health facilities as difficult, draining, and fruitless. Mental health professionals were viewed as ineffectual, although Mr. and Mrs. B. had always tried to do whatever was suggested for their daughter.

The present crisis involved their 18-year-old and only remaining child, Lisa. She had just told them that she thought she was pregnant by her boyfriend of 2 years and that they wanted to marry. Although she maintained the pregnancy was an accident, the worker understood it to be a disguised attempt by Lisa to distinguish herself from her sister and affirm her desire for life. At the same time, it was an attempt to give herself a purpose and identity in life where she saw little. The crisis, however, was related to the conflict between Lisa's solution to her problem and her mother's strong need to see just about everything that happened in the family as negative and herself as the destructive cause of it all. Unable to separate out what she was and was not responsible for, Mrs. B. could not develop a plan of action for the situation and was faced with her own rising panic. Evidence of the family's immobilization was the fact that Lisa had not as yet seen a doctor to determine for certain whether she was pregnant.

Most important for the present discussion is how the here-and-now focus on the crisis coupled with a clearly stated time limit had a freeing and mobilizing effect on this family. The worker began by reflecting to the family that the crisis seemed more related to how each saw his or her responsibility to the probable pregnancy rather than the pregnancy itself. While significant issues relating to life and death, and replacement or rebirth of a lost family member could have been discussed, the worker correctly decided to focus on the more pressing and currently debilitating struggle around separation and differentiation as it was being played out in this crisis. The family could then be helped to define the crisis area and begin to outline some steps that would facilitate a solution. The suggestion that the boyfriend be included since he was essential to any decision-making process helped to decrease Mrs. B.'s inflated sense of power and give some support to Lisa's and her father's different views of the problem.

When a time limit of up to five more sessions was suggested, Mr. and Mrs. B. looked as if a great weight had been lifted from their shoulders; it immediately allowed them to see this experience as different from the previous ones. They began to tell the worker how relieved they were that they would not have to come for an indefinite length of time and how pleased they were that the worker thought this was a problem that could be handled in a short period of time. Both indicated then how hesitant they had been to call, fearful that the whole round of endless and guilt-provoking sessions would begin all over again. They were also free to say how much they did not want to dig up the past events of their daughter's death, although with the time limit and present-oriented focus Mrs. B. could reflect on how difficult a year it had been. Mr. B. stated that he had told his wife that he believed they could handle this together and saw the suggestion of a time limit as support of his ability to do so. Lisa also experienced the time limit as differentiating this treatment contact from those concerning her sister and helped her to see it as constructive for her.

Very often when the treatment plan involves systems field work it is impossible to be specific at the beginning about when and where the appointments will be held and who will attend. However, if the treatment focus and work arena are outlined properly then the time limit can be understood in this context. The way in which this evolved in the Abrams case, previously discussed, exemplifies such an expectation.

The worker recognized with Mr. Abrams that he had been thrown off balance by the landlord's personal request for the rent and saw his present concerns as both how to handle the landlord and again stabilize his financial condition. Knowing also that Mr. A. needed some assurance that he would not be dispossessed (abandoned), she outlined the work ahead as follows: (1) they would discuss and work out such issues as how to handle the landlord; and (2) field visits would be made to two other agencies, specifically the Department of Public Assistance for temporary financial support and to an affiliated employment and vocational guidance agency to help with re-employment. When it was pointed out to Mr. A. that this would be accomplished in up to five sessions, he felt reassured that his crisis was being taken seriously. Although the specific dates of the appointments, where they would be located, and exactly who would attend would have to be planned as they went along, the treatment focus and time limit had helped to mobilize and support those ego strengths that Mr. A. had available to him.

When Quick Response
Is Not Applicable

No discussion of the beginning phase of Quick Response is complete without a consideration of those clients who would be best helped by some service other than Quick Response. Since no treatment modality is suitable for all clients, it is important to recognize early when some direction other than this is indicated. Nevertheless, we are here discussing exceptions to the rule since the majority of clients who apply for help are appropriately seen in Quick Response. Many practitioners, especially when first beginning, find the demands of a time limit and a defined treatment focus very difficult and are tempted to avoid the struggle by deciding that a particular client cannot be helped by Quick Response and needs another form of treatment—often long-term psychotherapy. Therefore, it is important that the determination of the inappropriateness of this treatment be made according to the following considerations.

The extent of a client's pathology does not determine the appropriateness of Quick Response since it is equally effective with severely disturbed clients as it is with well-adjusted clients in crisis. However, clients who are acutely decompensating or those who are so severely depressed that their minimal social functioning is impaired cannot be considered for this service. In all probability, these clients are not treated at a social service agency anyway, but are usually referred to a psychiatric hospital. In general, the client for a time-limited psychotherapy must be "possessed of sufficient ego strengths to be able to negotiate a treatment agreement and to tolerate a treatment schedule." (Mann, 1973, p. 17). Clients who are unable to manage this minimum requirement need to be considered for treatment other than Quick Response and the beginning process should be considered an evaluation period to determine what kind of help the client can use.

Just as it is impossible to determine the effectiveness of Quick Response by the extent of the client's pathology, so it is impossible to determine the treatment modality by the content of the client's problem. Cases, for example, that involve questions of child neglect or child placement are not automatically ruled out of Quick Response. These situations need to be evaluated like any other; the clients have asked for help at a given time because of a particular crisis. An evaluation of the disequilibrium that has led to their request for help and an understanding of the system that has failed to work will facilitate a defined treatment objective that, if accomplished, can make an important difference in the family's life. More treatment at the same or another resource may or may not be indicated at the conclusion of the Quick Response service; this must be evaluated at the point of termination. This evaluation will be discussed further in the chapter that deals with termination.

Sometimes the practitioner from another resource where the client has been involved wishes to refer him to a social service agency or a mental health facility for long-term psychotherapy. Usually the referring agency, such as a hospital, has helped the client through the crisis and cannot continue, but recommends ongoing treatment. Since the client is not requesting help at a point of crisis and has already had some form of brief therapy, Quick Response is often not appropriate and long-term treatment may, in fact, be indicated. As with any referral, however, the agency accepting the referral has a responsibility to make its own evaluation of the recommendation. Referrals are sometimes made for other than the stated reason: The client may not have used treatment but the referring worker fails to evaluate this; at times a case has gotten out of the worker's control and the referral is a response to this; or the client may be requesting more treatment as a way of avoiding termination. When clear indications are made for long-term psychotherapy, however, the client should bypass Quick Response and begin in the unit of the agency where it is offered.

Finally, there are some instances when the client contact is so brief that the beginning Quick Response process of uncovering the nature of the crisis, determining a treatment focus, and establishing a time limit is either not possible or counterindicated. While certain aspects of the beginning process may be present, the client is able in one session to get what she or he needs to move on alone toward resolution of the problem. Usually this occurs when the help needed involves clarification of an issue, support of a direction already undertaken, and/or referral to another resource for a service such as legal assistance, vocational guidance, or a senior citizens' program.

Chapter 3

MIDDLE PHASE AND TERMINATION

MIDDLE PHASE

Objectives

Although no phase of treatment is so strictly defined that movement from one to the next can be rigidly designated, there is a process that evolves from the beginning to the middle and through the end that needs to be understood. While certain generic elements are active throughout the treatment, each phase has its own particular features and purposes. The work of the beginning period has been discussed: meeting the client, using a diagnostic assessment to engage the client in the treatment work, establishing a treatment focus, and setting a time limit. The middle phase of the Quick Response treatment entails the continued exploration and development of the treatment focus in such a way as to facilitate the client's movement toward resolution of the present crisis. When the amount of time available is short the importance of confining the work to the material of the current crisis is vital. However, the practitioner's ability to determine what is relevant and what is not must depend on a clinical understanding of personality and family dynamics, along with a systems understanding of the social milieu within which the client/family operates.

Therapeutic Procedures and Interventions

Various therapeutic procedures can help with the work of this middle phase, and the choice of some procedures over others will depend on the needs of the client-situation constellation. While the worker's role is an active one, activity is never measured simply by the number of words spoken or interventions executed. The time-limited and crisis-oriented nature of Quick Response necessitates a defined and focused process and the worker's leadership responsibility lies in this direction. The movement of any therapeutic process comes from the interaction between the client/family's spontaneous productions and the practitioner's calculated responses; there are a number of therapeutic procedures and interventions that assist in this.

1. *Support* of the client's ego strengths is called for when they are used to facilitate problem resolution. Support, however, does not refer to direct praise but is rather a way of adding strength or lending weight to the client's own direction and, therefore, allowing for the maximum maintenance of her or his integrity. This can be accomplished in many ways but the worker must choose his or her moments purposefully: Interest may be expressed in a line of questioning developed by the client; reinforcement can be used when strict superego dictates are relaxed; and acceptance of the client's feelings may be stressed when their expression represents a new venture for him. Since often the most valuable therapeutic work is what the client is

able to do for himself, support techniques have the important added benefit of heightening the client's self-esteem.

2. *Exploration* of the individual's and family's thoughts, feelings, and behavior as they relate to the central issue is an important intervention.

    Reflection on the above organizes the client's productions, verbal and nonverbal, into a more relevant and meaningful whole.

    Clarification of intellectual confusions and affective distortions results from the above.

3. *Ventilation* allows the discharge of pent-up emotions, often with the release of associated memories. Its value lies mostly "in validating for the patient what it is that troubles him [rather] than in effecting any kind of quick cure. . . ." (Mann, 1973, p. 49)

4. *Patterns* are observed in the individual's or family's affective responses and modes of behavior.

5. *Connections* are made between current functioning and historical factors.

6. *Education* consists of the transmission of information that can range from psychological facts and family phenomena to community resources and procedures for utilizing them. The effectiveness of the educational effort depends upon the client being in a receptive state to hear the information and the information meeting both the client's present intellectual confusion and emotional need.

7. *Confrontation* is what Ackerman (1966) calls "'tickling the defenses.' This is a tactic of catching the family members by surprise by exposing dramatic discrepancies between their self-justifying rationalizations and their subverbal attitudes. He [the therapist] challenges empty cliches and static or pat formulae for meeting the problems of family living. He halts fruitless bickering over routine, external, or unimportant matters. . . . To counteract the tendency to substitute empty verbalisms for genuine emo-

tional interchange, he catalyzes in the members the urge to explore these dramatic contradictions between verbal utterances and bodily expression." (p. 97)

8. *Redirection* involves the worker's responsibility in time-limited treatment to maintain the focus of work on the issues of the current crisis and is accomplished by utilizing the above forms of intervention.

9. *Systems activity* includes the coordination of auxiliary services within one's own facility, the identification of appropriate community resources, advocacy efforts vis à vis other community resources on the client's behalf, obtaining or improving existing services from other community resources that the worker and client undertake jointly. These activities involve telephone contact, field visits, and meetings with personnel from other community resources.

In some cases all of these procedures are utilized, while in others only certain ones are needed. By the conclusion of the beginning phase it is often clear which interventive methods will be most beneficial to a particular client and the work of the middle period involves their execution. While systems activities helped Mr. Abrams re-establish his financial security and emotional equilibrium, these methods would have been counterindicated with the Rosenthal family, where the issues of loss and concerns around parenting were resolved, in part, by methods of confrontation. Nevertheless, both clients required supportive techniques along the way. The time-limited nature of Quick Response, coupled with the client's inevitable pull away from work on the present crisis, necessitates an emphasis on redirection and will be discussed more fully in the section dealing with resistances. The association of the current problems with past experiences and relevant historical facts, however, can lead to the affective release and broadened cognitive perspective often necessary to resolve the current crisis. It is for the worker to evaluate the client's movement in this light, respond selectively, and help the client connect this to the present.

Transference Phenomena in Quick Response

Although it is helpful to review these therapeutic procedures, it is important to remember that the real movement in any treatment process results from the proper interaction between the client and worker. As Dr. Strean states in *Clinical Social Work: Theory and Practice,* "The most important dimension in any change effort is how the recipient *experiences* the activity. The social worker may 'sustain', 'advise', 'reinforce' or be a 'social broker', but the client may and often does experience the social worker's activity in a way very different from that in which it was intended." (1978, p. 192) Dr. Strean continues, "The phenomena of 'transference' and 'countertransference' exist in every relationship between two or more people, professional or non-professional, and must be taken into account in every social-worker–client encounter. By 'transference' is meant the feelings, wishes, fears and defenses of the client deriving from reactions to significant persons in the past (parents, siblings, extended family, teachers), that influence his current perceptions of the social worker." (p. 193) For any treatment intervention to be successful, the practitioner must consider how his or her efforts are being experienced by the client and evaluate this in light of the transference. Subsequent actions must then take these observations into account. However, rather than review here generic principles of transference, those phenomena particular to Quick Response because of its crisis-oriented and time-limited nature need to be addressed. Issues of countertransference will be discussed in Chapter 5 on workers' adjustment to Quick Response.

PREDICTABLE CHANGES AND EFFECTS FROM TIME LIMIT.   In general, the increased vulnerability the client experiences during a crisis heightens both her or his positive and negative transferential feelings toward the person in authority and sharpens areas of residual ambivalence. Many elements of the beginning period stimulate positive transferential feelings and fantasies: the speed and sensitivity of the worker's availability; the immediate release of pressure that accompanies first telling about the crisis and the cognitive organization that often results; and the experience of the time limit on a conscious level as an indication of the worker's optimism that the client can be helped. However, as we move into the middle phase a number of phenomena occur simultaneously to heighten the negative transference. The time limit that earlier, on an unconscious level, jarred the client's infantile dependent fantasies and omnipotent desires now meets the focused work demands of the middle phase and adds fuel to an already smoldering fire. The person who earlier offered comfort and respite now holds out a certain expectation of continued work in a specific area of endeavor that is inevitably difficult and anxiety-provoking for the client. The worker is no longer experienced so positively; negative and ambivalent feelings, fantasies, and wishes are provoked. While progress may even be apparent, it can never be as swift and total as the client's wishes and infantile fantasies have promised. The time limit now contributes to a heightening of the ego functions of reality testing, contributing to a more realistic view of what can be accomplished and how the client will have to participate in the process. The negative transference is further stimulated since the worker may seem to be duplicating those significant people of the past who have disappointed, abandoned, and/or demanded too much. The client's conflict over his or her own sense of resourcefulness and independence may be further exacerbated and the negative transference heightened even more. For those who desired a more prolonged period of dependency, the focus on work runs counter to their unconscious agenda; and for those who enjoyed the distance that they imagined a time limit would afford, the increased expo-sure of the middle phase can be threatening.

Systems work can become even more complex because in addition to an operational understanding of the resource(s) involved and an evaluation of the client's ego strengths, nega-tive transferential reactions must also be considered. If, for example, the school district supervisor is the person with the real decision-making authority at a suspension hearing, then the Quick Response supervisor will also have to attend in order to create the necessary leverage. The effect this has on the client will vary depending upon the state of the transference. While earlier the supervisor's presence may have been seen as an indication of the worker's and the agency's willingness to pull out all the stops to help, the processes of the middle phase may have heightened the negative transferential feelings so that this action is instead taken as proof of the worker's ineffectiveness.

TRANSFERENCE WORK IN QUICK RESPONSE.   Although in long-term psychotherapy a fuller development and analysis of the transference is often desirable, the time limitation of Quick Response makes this impossible and requires certain responses in order to limit, contain, and use the transference reactions so that they enhance rather than impede the treatment progress. It is often preferable to help the client analyze the problematic transference reaction as it emerges between family members or between the client and a person within the crisis environment rather than between the worker and client. This not only minimizes the emphasis on the therapeutic relationship but also helps the client(s) to observe right then and there a contrib-uting factor to the current crisis and/or strengthen the natural support system available to help her or him resolve the crisis. Sometimes, however, it is necessary or even desirable to ana-lyze the transference phenomena within the therapeutic rela-tionship, and once this has been done the client should be helped to see how it applies to the current crisis. The most crucial aspect of how transference material is handled in Quick Response is that it must be defined by the boundaries of the present crisis and the meaning of the phenomena confined to the central issue. Any information gained from the analysis must be connected to the here and now of the treatment focus. Mann (1973) maintains that "Adherence to the central issue . . . will limit the area of regression in the transference." (p. 50)

Mrs. Jacobs, the client previously discussed whose crisis involved her decision about whether her adult daughter should return home to live, entered the middle phase of treatment and became increasingly angry at the worker's nonresponsiveness to her presentation of unrelated issues and his continued efforts to redirect the discussion to the treatment focus. While Mrs. J. agreed with the centrality of this issue her reactions became increasingly negative and she felt ignored and rejected. Much of this reaction was transferential and reflected a distorted view of mothering that caused Mrs. J. to expect any authority person to be ever-present and available. The worker's definition of and limitation on the work to be done was tantamount, in her view, to rejection. Realizing how this distortion contributed to Mrs. J.'s difficulty in saying no to her daughter, the worker reintroduced information previously presented by Mrs. J. about her relationship with her own mother and encouraged Mrs. J. to talk about how available and ever-ready her mother was for her. Mrs. J. readily presented her ambivalences when she spoke of how inhibited and responsible she felt because her mother never took responsibility for setting appropriate limits and saying no when necessary. The similarity between Mrs. J.'s relationship with her mother, what was happening with the worker, and her view of what she "owed" Angel was apparent to both and the work on the treatment focus could continue enriched by this use of the transferential reactions. The choice had been to relate these reactions to central issues of the crisis and the present aspects of the problem rather than emphasize the worker-client relationship.

Resistance

Although we have reviewed therapeutic procedures and discussed the phenomenon of transference as both emerge in the middle phase of treatment, basic to any change process is the client's resistance to change. The purpose of many transference reactions, in fact, is to allow the client to resist change (Strean, 1978, p. 202) and interventive techniques are needed to help resolve resistances. No matter how much a person wants to change, how uncomfortable she or he may be with the way things are, and how clearly she or he sees the direction to be taken, some opposition to progress is inevitable. As change is approached, resistance intensifies and the desire to retreat increases. A family may cling to counterproductive alliances and destructive myths already exposed. The negative interaction between a client and the representative of a particular community resource may persist even though the harmful consequences are apparent to both. Resistance to change results from the client's/family's/system's fears about change, smoldering angers that are unexpressed yet preserved, defenses that need to be maintained, and secondary gains that are hard to give up.

Although resistances exist throughout treatment, much of what has been discussed as particular to the middle phase of Quick Response contributes to their intensification during this period: The optimism of the beginning phase alerts the client that the status quo is threatened; the continued attention to the treatment focus stimulates ambivalences about change; the establishment of a time limit of up to six sessions makes it clear that if change is to occur it will be now, not some abstract point in the future; and, finally, the client begins to sense what the process of change will demand. Resistances are expressed in numerous ways and the worker's attention to them must not subside until treatment has ended.

The time limitation of Quick Response precludes the possibility of allowing the resistances to develop slowly and emerge in a more full-blown state. During this middle period the worker must be quick to take note of the resistances where they appear, actively tease them out into the open, and even uproot them when they are more disguised and hidden. Resistances make their appearances in a Quick Response case with the same variety typical to any treatment modality. The client/ family may be late for an appointment, forget to pay the fee, be compliant or defiant toward whatever is said, or have no information to offer about the problem under discussion. Group silences, newly formed negative alliances, and disguised references to the worker are all common. Sudden failure to implement plans made in reference to another resource or attendance at a community meeting without the necessary papers does occur. The identification and understanding of these resistances affords the practitioner rich opportunity to exercise her or his creative energies.

TIME AS A FOCAL POINT OF RESISTANCE.   Even though resistances do find numerous avenues of expression, the impact of the time structure in Quick Response often becomes a focal point for resistances. The client suddenly wants to "change" the appointment "time," is not "on time" with the fee payment, questions whether six sessions is "enough time" or even "too much time," or acts as if he or she has "all the time" in the world by introducing every problem other than the crisis concern. References are made to the practitioner's use of time; you must be "short of time," "your time" is limited, you are too busy, I know you have to spread "your time thin," you don't have any "more time" for me. As the actuality of separation becomes more pressing, transference reactions may become even more the vehicle for resistances. When the client's willingness to change becomes so interwoven with his or her ambivalent feelings about separation, whatever is problematic in the separation has also been a contributing factor in the crisis that brought her or him for help.

Toward the end of Mrs. Henderson's third appointment she began for the first time to ventilate feelings of loneliness and isolation as a single parent, and to reflect on how unsure she often felt with the many decisions she had to make. She complained that her mother, in-laws, and now the school all failed to offer her the support she desperately needed, and that they were instead demanding and victimizing of her. Although pleased with the worker's interest and acceptance of what she was saying, as the session came to an end Mrs. H. began for the first time to make reference to the shortness of the treatment time and timidly asked for more. With this request her demeanor began to change and a plaintive quality entered her voice. When asked how she felt about the time limit, Mrs. H. instead described the worker as busy and unavailable, and as more powerful and controlling than she who was now weak and forced to accept whatever was offered. Her voice contained a mixture of passivity and resentment. As soon as Mrs. H. had risked expressing her dependency wishes, she had to make the worker into a person who condemned and limited them as her mother had done originally and many others had subsequently. Ambivalent feelings about dependency caused her to enlist the condemnation of others in order to keep them in check. The request to extend the time became a disguised effort to get the worker to "kick her out."

When Mrs. H. came to the next session late and began by saying that she knew the worker must be angry at her, there was ample material for a continuation of this discussion. The crises that had resulted from the school conference became clearer. Mrs. H. had gone to the conference secretly wishing for some support from the principal and guidance counselor for her efforts as a single parent. However, her own negative judgement of these wishes caused her to readily join with them in a condemnation of her abilities. Her own harsh judgement of herself made it impossible to evaluate their behavior critically and to assert herself appropriately. Helping the client to understand what was meant by her request for more time and her reactions to the worker's availability, rather than complying with it or brushing it aside, contributed to important movement on the crisis issue.

The continued work of this middle phase is marked by an increase of negative transferential phenomena, heightened resistances, and some more reaction to the time limit. The extent and timing of the emergences of these processes will naturally vary from one case to another.

TERMINATION

As treatment enters the termination phase, usually around the fifth session, the impending separation takes on increased importance. Although the dynamics of any specific ending are determined by the client's situation, the relationship that has developed, and the tasks that have been proposed, certain universal conflicts have the potential for arising as the separation and termination are anticipated. The fact that the relationship began at a crisis point, the work was mutually defined and focused, and the time structured to heighten awareness of a beginning, middle, and end, all contribute to creating a more significant therapeutic relationship than ordinarily happens within so short a time.

Universal Phenomena

The process of separation from someone who has understood and been helpful and the termination of a relationship that began in the midst of a crisis often evokes strong feelings in all parties involved. Many people have difficulty with the sense of loss that is so often a part of this process and experience the many feelings and thoughts that accompany the various facets of the separation process in less than a clear and straightforward way. In order to guard against what is often a distorted view of the process, people may behave in characteristically defensive ways. Memories of past experiences of loss through separation, rejection, or death are sometimes reawakened and unresolved grief is stirred up. Unresolved ambivalent feelings toward present and past love objects can be reenacted within the therapeutic relationship, leading to the existence of conflictual feelings, thoughts, and behavior. A wide range of feelings are possible at this point: anger at the worker, who is seen as unavailable and rejecting; blame toward him or her for not offering all that the client's unconscious fantasies had promised; anger over the limitations inevitably experienced; guilt about these angry feelings and fantasies; sadness at the thought of missing the person; appreciation for the help received; excitement and a sense of adventure about being on one's own; guilt over these feelings; fear over one's ability to manage alone.

Depending upon the maturational level of the client, the process of separation will provoke anxiety around different unresolved issues. Questions of trust vs. mistrust may be couched in accusations of rejection and abandonment, omnipotent fantasies to explain the rejection, and fears of helplessness. Issues of dependency versus independency include fears and angers over the loss of nurturing both real and imagined, and questions about competency and accomplishment when on one's own. Conflicts around activity versus passivity are expressed in fears about taking the initiative and guilt over autonomous behavior. Termination of treatment may arouse concerns about intimacy as a couple faces themselves alone with each other. Although family members experience these same concerns around separation, since they continue together after treatment anxieties are often expressed as to how the worker's absence will affect their continued family functioning.

Termination as a Part of the Treatment Process

Termination is a part of an ongoing treatment process and, therefore, what has come before will affect what happens at the end. The quality of the relationship, its intensity, and its effectiveness over the previous sessions will influence how separation is experienced. If a certain risk taking has been encouraged, met with acceptance, and even proved beneficial, feelings around separation that are experienced as risky are more likely to be expressed. In contrast, if the relationship has unfortunately been one in which the client(s) has not felt free to express her or his angry and critical feelings toward the worker, the lack of avenues previously constructed for the expression of these negative feelings will make it doubly difficult during the separation and termination process. Only if all family members have been treated with a real sense of equality can there be full participation in the termination process.

The methods of intervention utilized during the middle phase also influence the termination process. If, for example, systems activity dominates and treatment time is spent largely on advocacy meetings and environmental manipulation, fewer of the client's preconscious feelings and fantasies will emerge. Therefore, the feelings that are available about separation from the worker and termination from treatment will be more superficial. If, on the other hand, methods such as ventilation and confrontation were used, then preconscious material, ambivalent transferential feelings, and maturational conflicts will be stimulated and a more intense and complex termination process is likely.

Finally, how active separation issues are and how they relate to the central issue of the crisis influence the force with which the middle phase ushers in the termination process. For example, the intensity of the separation process during the termination phase will be considerable for the Rosenthal family because of the nature of their crisis and the interventive techniques used during the middle phase. Since Mr. Rosenthal's death is central to their family crisis, issues of separation and loss have been a constant theme and the use of such techniques as ventilation, establishment of connections, and confrontation have helped to uncover and expose much in this area. In contrast, while some time was spent on Mr. Abrams' feelings of loss centered around being laid off, his fear of eviction, and his sense of life alone without his mother, the thrust of the work was to strengthen Mr. Abrams' defenses rather than stir up conflictual material about separation and loss. Consequently, systems activity that included a meeting at the Department of Welfare, an appointment at an affiliated employment agency, and preparation for his meeting with the landlord accounted for much of the middle phase. Therefore, while there are certain dynamics generic to the termination phase, the work of the middle period must also be considered in order to anticipate how the termination process will be experienced.

Avoidance Issues

THE WORKER.   Even with the clarity of a termination date, a strong desire to avoid this part of treatment can be present as much for the practitioner as the client. If unable to come to terms with this difficulty, the worker will inevitably join the client in avoiding the termination process. Being human also, the worker is susceptible to the same pain, ambivalent feelings, and unresolved conflicts associated with separation. Positive feelings for the client/family and an investment in a job well done will naturally lead to some feelings of sadness and loss. Mann (1973) points out, "The doubts of the therapist as to his effectiveness are again readily aroused at this point when the patient takes refuge once more in symptoms, distressing complaints, or disturbing behavior. At the same time, the therapist must confront his own ambivalences in respect to the same conflicts within himself as these are exposed by the patient." (p. 59) Discomfort and even guilt with feelings of relief in anticipation of ending with a client who has been particularly difficult may lead to an avoidance of a real process. The structure of a time limit that makes the ending foreseeable and non-negotiable leaves little room for delay in dealing with the important issues of this phase of treatment. The rapidity with which each case ends and the sheer number of endings at any one time in a Quick Response caseload means that the worker must come to terms with her or his avoidance in order to provide a strong leadership position.

Theoretical formulations and teaching efforts have often been concentrated on beginnings and middles out of a keen awareness that without a proper beginning and a productive middle where resistances are recognized, a real ending is too often replaced by a premature or aborted one in which the client abruptly leaves. This concentration, although quite legitimate, has conveniently fit individual and collective desires to avoid the pain and conflicts so often involved with separation. However, to execute Quick Response successfully means to come to terms with feelings and activities that would otherwise lead to an avoidance of the separation and termination process and a neglect of the issues of this phase of treatment.

THE CLIENT.   Ways of avoiding separation and termination fall into four categories. The client (and worker) *denies* termination by acting as if the work together will continue and no references are made to separation or a final appointment. The termination point may be acknowledged but its importance or any feelings about it denied. Another method commonly used is *regression* to a previous way of behaving or to a symptom seen earlier in treatment that now re-emerges perhaps in an even more extreme form. A physical symptom suddenly reoccurs around the fifth appointment or family members are fighting again in an old familiar way about an issue that had seemed to be resolved. The desire for *flight* in order to avoid the separation process can escalate very quickly if clues go unattended and the client is not helped to verbally express feelings rather than having to act them out. While in its most extreme form the client flees treatment, a milder form may involve lateness for an appointment or failure to remember something the client had previously been quite involved in discussing. Finally, words and behavior may be used to demonstrate how much the client *needs* your continued help, and thus must insist that treatment not end. New problems or new facets of a problem may suddenly be introduced and may even seem quite urgent. If one is solved another might quickly appear. The message is clear that you are indispensable (Hoffmann and Remmel, 1975; Mann, 1973; Strean, 1978).

Since the client prefers to express his or her feelings about ending treatment and separation from the practitioner through one or more of these disguised forms, an active stance is needed during this phase of treatment to counteract this avoidance and to help with a more open and direct expression. When working with a family, one or two members may be more direct than the others; however, at times the entire family presents a united front of resistance. The interventive techniques previously discussed are available to use appropriately to combat the client's wish to avoid the termination process. The separation is from the real relationship that has developed, from the symbolic one it represents, and also from the treatment process. The dynamics of each are interwoven in many respects and distinct in others. Which aspects of this are most important and how deeply they need to be investigated will again depend on the client/family and the dynamics of the crisis that precipitated the need for help. Simultaneously the worker must keep a critical eye on his own inclinations to avoid termination and question whether he or she is moving away from the complexities of this phase of treatment.

ANGRY FEELINGS AND TERMINATION.   Usually these feelings are the ones initially most difficult to express (and for the worker to hear) and avoidance maneuvers are attempts to deal with them. Whatever mutuality the client felt originally in the agreement to a time limit has long since been overruled by anxious feelings about separation and termination. The time may now seem too long, too short, or just right. He may agree, disagree, or go along with it, but usually feels to some extent imposed upon by the worker. An angry component is expressed in each form of avoidance discussed. While denial may serve many purposes, the client refuses to hear and wipes out what has been said about ending. Regression indicates to the worker that his or her efforts have been to no avail and flight from treatment leaves the worker without a client. Neediness may seem to indicate the client's love and admiration but since the treatment objective has been in some measure to restore self-sufficiency, this expression contains a message of failure. Anger can be used as a cover feeling to hide less acceptable feelings such as fear, loss, or grief. It can accompany and is often integral to the push-and-pull of ambivalences experienced around separation. Often cognitive distortions about separation cannot be clarified until the angry feelings that mask them are recognized. This anger can be an entry point to what is central to the termination process as well as to the substance of it.

The Rosenthal family came for their fifth appointment in an obvious state of regression; Mrs. R. had to push everyone into the room, Sara was angry and stomping, Evelyn was tearfully clinging, and Henry was hiding with his baseball. Mrs. R. began quickly and defensively to explain how she would not let the children stand in her way if, by chance, she decided to marry Mr. Abbott. She was quick to add that she had no immediate plans but she wanted them to know she would not let them stop her. The scene about to unfold was typical of the beginning of treatment; Sara was ready to grab the bait and respond belligerently to her mother by threatening to leave home. Henry had pushed his chair into a corner and was seemingly engrossed in his baseball and Evelyn, who had for some time sat straight in her own chair, now had herself neatly draped over Mom, who was trying to extricate herself so she could "answer" Sara. The message to the worker was clearly that they were back to the beginning and could not possibly end. Efforts to discuss their feelings about separation at the end of the fourth session, when references had been made to how improved their situation was and how much more intact they felt as a family, had been pushed aside. Anger and fear about treatment ending and feelings of sadness and loss at leaving the worker were so disguised that any attempts made to pick up on them were unsuccessful. However, by the beginning of the fifth session the message was loud and clear.

The worker responded to this display by stating calmly that it seemed as if their work together had not been very successful, thus focusing the family off themselves and closer to the real issues of their feelings about the treatment. As everyone responded to this—the children agreeing and Mrs. R. politely disagreeing—the worker joined the children by indicating that the evidence seemed clear. Mrs. R. gave up her pretense and referred also to her disappointment.

Once closer to the point, the worker could then wonder how they felt toward her not coming through for them. What they then said sounded reminiscent of how they had spoken about Mr. R.'s leaving them and Mrs. R.'s ambivalences about being a single parent. As they ventilated their feelings and perceptions, the anger decreased and they could slowly begin to explore their powerful feelings about separation and termination. Naturally, this discussion constituted a major portion of the fifth and sixth sessions.

While it is helpful with some clients to express their anger, and then to investigate it and understand what is underneath, this is not always possible and other less direct means can be beneficially used.

Unconsciously, Mr. Abrams experienced separation as a recapitulation of the abandonment he had felt when his mother died and employed fairly rigid defenses to keep his rage in check. To expect him to express and explore these feelings would not only be impossible in so short a time, but was counterindicated in light of the treatment focus and direction undertaken. However, his need to keep angry feelings so tightly controlled influenced his separation from the worker as it had affected him in his current crisis. During the fifth appointment he became both ingratiating and needy, even attempting to flee treatment prematurely by indicating that he preferred not to come for his last appointment. His genuine appreciation was tainted by his angry and resentful feelings because he perceived the worker as also abandoning him. His neediness was proof she was leaving him in a lurch. Since this was truly out of Mr. A.'s awareness and it would have been counterproductive to try to deal directly with these issues, the worker accepted Mr. A.'s thanks and added how, in general, endings can be difficult, even seem incomplete or a bit aggravating. The message was received by Mr. A. because he then spoke about how upset he had been when laid off his job. As Mr. A. was given permission indirectly to express some of his angry feelings, a discussion about this aspect of separation became possible.

DRESS REHEARSAL.   Although the time limit has built into the client's (and worker's) consciousness an awareness of termination, and the emergence of crisis-related separation issues reinforces the definiteness of ending, more can still be done to minimize the client's avoidance. While in actuality separation is never completed until treatment is ended and the participants have gone their separate ways, the more real the client experiences the ending to be, the more substantially will her or his reactions to separation emerge, and vice versa. Encouraging the client to think ahead about handling the problem after termination reminds the client that the worker will not be around in the very near future. This pushes the client to anticipate how it will be and to evaluate her or his own resources to deal with the problem alone. Additionally, this dress rehearsal educates the client about reactions to be expected after termination and can minimize their off-balancing potential.

After the Rosenthals had begun to talk more directly about separation the worker asked them to think about how they would handle this typical defensive behavior when it occurs after termination. Following the family's unified protest that it would never happen again, Sara was first to recognize that they would of course do their "thing" again and explained very realistically how each of them gets defensive when they feel another is "deserting them." Mrs. R. supported her evaluation and Henry was first to recommend a way of dealing with their problem by suggesting a family meeting like they have had in treatment. The discussion continued, anticipating the various nuances of the problem and trying on different solutions for size and wearability.

Review and Evaluation

Finally, as part of the termination process, the client/family and worker need together to review and evaluate what has transpired during treatment: review of the state of affairs when help was requested and the crisis issues explored; reiteration of the substance of the crisis and the family members' individual and collective participation in coping with the problem; and a recapitulation of the systems actively utilized. An evaluation of what changes were effected, tasks accomplished, and work that remains brings them up to the present. Emphasis on strengthening the client's cognitive hold on this crisis period so that treatment is terminated with an intellectual overview increases the ability to cope in the future. The client's maximum participation should be encouraged, with the worker acting mainly as a facilitator. This review and evaluation also allows for some development of closure to the experience, thus furthering the separation process. Discussion of future planning helps the client to visualize himself or herself without treatment.

Planned Ending
in Less Than Six Sessions

Since the Quick Response contract is for "up to six sessions," treatment sometimes terminates in less than six. This refers, however, to an ending mutually agreed upon by all participants with sufficient time allotted for an appropriate termination process, not to an unplanned ending because the client prematurely interrupts treatment in order to avoid the issues of separation. For example, by the third or fourth session the treatment focus could have been sufficiently resolved, with the designated tasks accomplished so that the crisis is well on its way to resolution. If the client's/family's functioning has returned to a balanced state and the work of separation from the relationship has begun, termination is then indicated. At least one session is needed after this decision in order to work on the elements of the termination process previously discussed. If a client is hesitant to allow for this, the worker should be suspicious about whether termination is really indicated or if the purpose is to flee from the termination process.

The majority of clients will want to end appropriately after the Quick Response sequence, having resolved the crisis that motivated them to seek help and again feeling sufficiently balanced in their functioning. Those clients who attempt to prolong treatment by avoidance measures such as neediness and regression will talk less about continuing as the separation issues are more directly exposed and confronted and, thus, the real reasons for continuing are being resolved. Included in this group are those clients who are doing well and report no specific problems but want to continue because of a fear that without treatment things will again fall apart.

Cases to Be Transferred

There is, however, a third group whose request to continue has a purpose and validity that should be considered. These clients have used Quick Response to resolve their current crisis and as an outgrowth of the treatment are now eager to work on a more "chronic or persistent" problem that they may or may not have been aware of prior to the crisis. Hoffman and Remmel (1975) state, "Unlike the group of clients who resist terminating, clients in this group present problems which are longstanding and easily identified." (p. 267) But to maintain the time-limited structure and allow the work of crisis resolution to be effective, the termination process with these clients must be handled the same as with other groups of clients, and the discussion about and decision to continue cannot be considered until the end of the Quick Response period as part of the review and evaluation process. A more accurate view of this issue of continuation is that a significant segment of work has been completed and the decision involves beginning work on another, at times even related, problem. To reflect this and simultaneously maintain the integrity of the Quick Response process, the client ends with the Quick Response worker and transfers to continued service to begin a new period of treatment, either open-ended or time-limited. The success of a transfer process depends upon the work of separation having been sufficiently tackled. If not, for example, the worker may unintentionally try to hold back the client and/or set up a competitive situation between Quick Response and continued service.

Mrs. Hernandez requested help because of a problem with her 13-year-old daughter, Sheryl. Although the eldest of four children, Sheryl was considered the least intelligent and least ambitious in a family where both were critical. Mrs. H., an Haitian immigrant who had been divorced for many years, worked hard to raise and support her family. It was important to her that they do well in school since she saw this as the vehicle for upward mobility. All did average to superior work except for Sheryl, who had always been a marginal student. Mrs. H. ran a tight ship, expecting each child to carry a very full load of responsibility. Sheryl shared least in the family warmth and security and was clearly the family scapegoat. She was seen as simple because she liked to do the domestic chores in a family where this was considered demeaning and the unspoken question was whether or not she was mentally retarded. When Sheryl was a small child Mrs. H. had gone from one agency to another in order to get help with her marginal school performance. Even though all children were currently in a better school district than ever before, Sheryl's performance had not improved and Mrs. H. still centered on this.

Recently, while doing the cleaning, Sheryl had accidentally broken a vase of great value to her mother (precipitating event). This had reinforced Mrs. H.'s view of Sheryl as lacking in responsibility and as overly dependent on her, and it intensified how "stuck" she felt (precipitant). An earlier incident during the summer, involving Sheryl's inability to manage her allowance had set the stage (emotional hazard), and Mrs. H. feared Sheryl would always be a burden to her. The underlying conflict involved an individual and family system that reinforced Mrs. H.'s strong need to deny her own and the children's dependency needs. Emphasis was on pseudo-independent functioning with little room for more dependent and playful feelings. Sheryl was the one who threatened to upset this and the precipitating event was more than Mrs. H. could handle.

The Hernandez family used the Quick Response sequence to evaluate and confront Sheryl's serious school problem and simultaneously to minimize the scapegoating phenomenon in the family. A systems approach that involved meetings with the family, school, and worker helped to diagnose a serious reading and math deficiency that Sheryl had had since the early grades. Not only could plans then be made for a special remedial tutoring program, but the question of Sheryl's intellectual capacity could more clearly be addressed. The treatment focus supported Mrs. H.'s positive desire to help Sheryl, reinforced her in-charge position in the family, and minimized her fears of Sheryl's perpetual dependency. As the scapegoating phenomenon lessened, the other children felt less threatened that they might be next, and less guilty about their actions toward their sister. Sheryl became more outspoken, more self-assertive, and less devious in her angry expressions.

Although the Quick Response work had not specifically focused on the problematic ways in which dependency needs were channeled in the Hernandez family, aspects of the dependency-independence conflict were touched upon and discussed. After the pertinent separation issues of the termination process had evolved, and as part of the review and evaluation period, Mrs. H. brought up the issue of her difficulty expressing her needs to others and getting and giving comfort. She saw the same pattern in varying ways with the children and had been thinking about whether this was a problem they should now try to work on. Once this possibility was opened up, a fuller family discussion led to a joint decision for continued treatment. This family had used Quick Response to resolve their crisis in a way that armed them with better coping mechanisms for the future. While they certainly could have terminated then and have been in a stronger position as a result of the treatment, they now felt ready to work on a more chronic individual and family problem.

Follow-up Appointment

Another alternative at termination is to set up a follow-up appointment with the client for 3 months after the last appointment. However, this must be used discriminatingly and not as a blanket alternative in Quick Response cases, because the establishment of a follow-up appointment can undermine the dynamic impact of a clear and definite termination point. Also the suggestion of a follow-up appointment may be experienced by the client as a vote of no confidence in his ability to manage without treatment and, if so, would counter those Quick Response principles that emphasize the temporary and crisis nature of the client's dilemma and that utilize available ego strengths to enable him to cope. Finally, it is often important that if help is again needed the client take the initiative in seeking it, and the follow-up may be experienced as negating this.

However, there are select situations when a follow-up

appointment can be useful because other considerations out-weigh these counterindications. When a midway point is needed between the dependency allowed in treatment and the demands of independent functioning after termination, a fol-low-up appointment can symbolically provide this. Secondly, when the work of Quick Response has helped to re-establish the homeostasis but the nature of the underlying conflict and the resources available to cope with it make the balance uncer-tain, a follow-up appointment provides a re-entry point per-haps before life is again in disarray. This planned re-entry may be needed, for example, around a particular occasion or transi-tion point that the worker can anticipate will be difficult for the client.

Occasionally a client will telephone prior to the follow-up appointment to cancel, often indicating how well things are going and questioning the need for the appointment. It is best to hold to the decision for a follow-up and use the appointment time to understand this cancellation request. If things are fine, sharing this and understanding the reservations about doing this can be helpful. If the wish to cancel was for some other reason, the follow-up appointment allows more room for in-vestigation.

REAPPLICATION

In order for a social service agency to be truly responsive to the needs of its population, service must not only be deliv-ered quickly and designed to meet the crisis and systems nature of the problem, but it must be available to clients as often as needed. The concepts of Quick Response and the view of an agency with a revolving front door are theoretically comple-mentary. Once intervention is viewed as specific to a particular crisis and time-limited, the realization that a client/ family may very well need help again at another point in its evolution is entirely consistent and it is important that the request for help be seen as a positive and constructive step, not as proof per se of the ineffectiveness of the previous treatment. Both client and worker must recognize that strength lies in knowing when to seek help, not in how frequently or infrequently it is used. With the enormous pressure on families today, coupled with the increasing disappearance of the extended family network, the social service agency has become the resource to which many now turn periodically for the help and support once offered by the structure of the extended family.

Chapter 4

OPERATIONAL IMPLEMENTATION OF QUICK RESPONSE

Whatever the form of psychotherapy, the design of the delivery system will determine how consistent actual service is with the theoretical framework of the therapy. An agency's delivery organization for a traditional intake service and transfer to long-term treatment invariably operates in ways that contradict the conceptual basis of Quick Response. The detailed review in Chapter 1 of just such a system highlighted the many ways in which the operational structure designed for one kind of practice conflicts with the objectives of another. A more thorough understanding of Quick Response now clarifies even further the extent of this incompatibility. Recognition of how inextricably linked are structure and practice explains why the development of Quick Response treatment necessitated simultaneous development of a delivery system designed to support it. The organization used to extrapolate the treatment of one client into a functioning service for a larger agency population has to be consistent with and serve to facilitate the clinical concepts of Quick Response.

Even though basic theoretical principles will always require certain operational considerations, variations in the circumstances and settings within which Quick Response operates necessitate some differences. Jewish Family Service's delivery organization can serve as a model for other social service agencies but adjustments have to be made for such things as the size of the agency staff and client population. Even though the basic design of the service remains intact, changes must also be made for the unique demands of a particular setting. For example, since many of the referrals to a school guidance department are not self-referrals but come from teachers and reflect some problem within the school system, the increased systems activity that will usually occur at the beginning of treatment must be incorporated into the design of that Quick Response program. Consequences stemming from the fact that often the doctor and not the patient initiates referral to the hospital social service department must also be considered when that system is designed. The many applications of Quick Response will be discussed in Chapter 6, but for now a closer look at the system established at Jewish Family Service will illuminate how theoretical considerations are translated into practical application. Naturally, basic Quick Response principles form the foundation for the operational system that provides delivery of this service.

THE QUICK RESPONSE UNIT

Since worker availability is at the heart of Quick Response, an agency has to concern itself with a system that enables a worker to be available to see the new client, continue with the one already being seen, and still provide coverage for those potential clients from the community about to request help. While in the past an agency's front doors could be closed when caseloads were full and time was no longer available, an open-door policy now becomes central to the operation of Quick Response. This new system must allow for the same flexibility about the arrangement of time and place throughout the duration of the case as was given at the beginning. Since systems activity is integral to this service, time must be freed up sufficiently to schedule blocks of time in the field. Workers no longer can operate in isolation from each other with no sense of joint activity or shared responsibility. For example, coverage has to be provided in the office for the new applicant while other workers are in the field.

A Quick Response unit is composed of a group of workers whose primary responsibility is to the delivery of a Quick Response service. A constant rotation of time-limited cases means time is continually being freed up so workers can begin with new applicants. Rather than each worker relating only to clients and a supervisor, the unit allows for more contact among peers and sharing of work responsibilities. It expands the possible ways in which work can be distributed and absorbed. Information, also, is easier to disperse and more readily shared within a group. This is especially important since the increased systems activity of Quick Response necessitates more familiarity with a wide range of community resources.

UNIT TASKS

Although it is artificial to divide Quick Response processes into segmented tasks, it helps in understanding how the unit's activities are structurally arranged. Briefly, they can be divided into three areas:

1. In-agency activity, including telephone/walk-in reception, office interviews, and the coordination of auxiliary services
2. Field activity, including home visits and systems activity
3. Community outreach

In-Agency Activity

TELEPHONE/WALK-IN RECEPTION.   Just as this is the beginning point with the client, the unit's responsibility for all new applications—whether by telephone, walk-in, or referral—is the hub of the wheel that makes up the unit's operations. All new requests for service are received by a Quick Response worker and although some of these do not evolve into Quick Response cases for reasons previously cited, the majority of them are absorbed into the unit. The system works simply: whenever an applicant telephones or walks in requesting help, the Quick Response worker on coverage that day immediately takes the call or sees the applicant. The agency's application form is filled out from information spontaneously presented by the client and does not interfere with professional exchange. Information still lacking is obtained at the end of the discussion. Whether the next step with the client is an appointment or further telephone activity, the worker who has begun continues with the client until the completion of the Quick Response activity. Carrying mostly Quick Response cases makes time available for new clients because the Quick Response sequence is continually ending with others.

Naturally the volume of new applications varies according to the size and setting of the agency, but when the number of new monthly applicants is sufficient for a unit of at least 10 workers, two are assigned daily to telephone/walk-in coverage. In smaller offices one worker provides coverage with a backup person available as needed. Schedules must be completely free this day for this assignment alone so that the new client can be met with maximum flexibility. When, how long, with whom, and where to see the client are decided according to the particular needs of that client and situation. The worker's options must be open to begin that day in the office, to make a home visit, or to set up a family conference for later that day. Consequently, the assignment is for a full day of coverage so that there is sufficient time to follow through on a plan without conflicting with previously scheduled appointments.

Mr. Jacobs telephoned the agency at 10:30 a.m. and spoke with Mrs. Spitz, the Quick Response worker assigned that day to telephone/walk-in coverage. Mr. J., 35 years old and single, lived in a rooming house, worked sporadically, and had a history of drug abuse. He stated that he was depressed after a recent fight with his girlfriend and described feelings of increasing disorientation. He had no connection at that point with any other treatment facility. After discussing his need to be seen immediately, Mr. J. decided to take a taxi to the office since he did not want Mrs. S. to make a home visit; he arrived about 1:00 p.m. Since Mrs. Spitz was on coverage for the full day, her need to follow through with Mr. Jacobs did not conflict with any previously scheduled appointments.

Examples such as this are many and the importance of availability at point of application cannot be emphasized enough. In fact, not only is the assignment for a full day of coverage, but even lunch hours are staggered so that the client does not have to wait, come back, or call again.

In a setting where the volume of telephone applications is high and the unit has more than four workers, it is helpful to have a room specifically set aside for telephone/walk-in coverage. This substantially facilitates the coordination of activity among the workers assigned that day to coverage. When they are all aware of the total volume of work as it comes in and share responsibility, fewer gaps in planning occur and better service is achieved. If one worker is busy with a call or client the other knows it and can plan accordingly. The physical proximity encourages professional exchange on the spot about a case or resource and emphasizes the importance of what workers have to offer each other.

Miss Furst had worked at the agency for only 6 weeks and was paired on telephone coverage with a more experienced worker to help her learn the job. A call from a young woman who sounded suicidal was put through to her. Although Miss F. was able to evaluate this as well as is possible on the telephone, she was anxious with the circumstances and made more so by a realistic lack of information about hospital facilities in the area. However, her co-worker's presence helped her considerably in the situation. Their both being in the same room enabled her to immediately discuss the situation with another professional, Mr. Ginsburg, and set the direction needed to carry it through to an appropriate conclusion. First he suggested important clarifying questions Miss F. needed to ask. These questions led to the identification of a neighbor in the next apartment who Mr. Ginsburg then called. Her help was enlisted to immediately take the young woman to the nearest hospital emergency room, where Miss Furst arranged for a psychiatric evaluation. The competence with which this crisis was met was enhanced by the coordinated work of two workers, which was made possible because of their physical proximity in the telephone coverage room.

The telephone room becomes the hub of the unit: It not only facilitates informal exchange of information about community resources, new programs and procedures, and what personnel to contact; it also provides a central place to keep resource files, bulletin boards, and manuals. Those not on coverage often come by to see how busy it is and to offer help when needed. Rather than having to wait to be told what to do, workers are encouraged by this structure to participate actively in the distribution of the work, to function independently and to support their peers.

OFFICE INTERVIEW.   Even though it is just as likely that the client will be seen in the field as in the office, the office interview will be considered first since it is a part of in-agency activity. The aspect most relevant to this operation is the scheduling of appointments. Other than the structuring of telephone/walk-in coverage and some community outreach work, the Quick Response worker's schedule is open to allow the greatest flexibility in appointment scheduling. How far in advance an appointment is made, as well as the frequency and amount of time per appointment cannot be predetermined by a schedule, but is allowed to vary according to what is needed in each particular case. Therefore, the unit's operational system leaves the length and frequency of office interviews to be determined within the context of the case and considered as treatment issues. Rather than using interview count as a way of evaluating the unit's or a worker's productivity, other factors such as the amount of used or open time need to be considered.

COORDINATION OF AUXILIARY SERVICES.   Whether Quick Response operates as the primary service within a social casework agency or as an auxiliary service in another host setting, multiple services are often housed under one roof and at times have to be integrated with each other. This is entirely consistent with a Quick Response approach, since resolution of the problem that brings the client for help is often enriched and sometimes only possible through a combination of services that addresses itself to different facets of the problem. Contributory factors in the precipitating crisis often involve external environmental as well as internal emotional forces, concrete as well as psychological elements. Examples of auxiliary services are financial assistance, homemaker service, psychiatric consultation, legal aid, and vocational consultation. These are usually easier and quicker to obtain if they are part of the agency; this circumvents the need to seek them in the community at large. Since the services are under the same umbrella, the Quick Response worker has more control over their operation, can make better use of them, and can avoid many of the complications that arise with interagency activity.

Mr. Rogers, a 50-year-old taxi driver, requested help with $100 in traffic tickets he had to pay in order to get his license reinstated. He indicated that the agency was his last resource and that the longer he could not work the more in debt he was getting. The emotional hazard had been the realization recently that the relationship with his girlfriend was going nowhere. This upset had affected his driving and led to the traffic tickets. The core conflict revolved around a longstanding sense of loss and abandonment over not seeing his children for 10 years. Although the Quick Response worker related to the emotional issues involved, enabling him to return to work as soon as possible was essential to helping Mr. Rogers. After a realistic evaluation that indeed he had no way of paying these tickets, the Quick Response worker agreed that the agency would give him this money. Discussion stemming from Mr. Rogers' request that this be a loan rather than a grant became an important aspect of the treatment process. Therefore, in more than one way, the financial assistance was crucial to the effectiveness of the Quick Response service.

Procedurally, the Quick Response worker first evaluates the need for auxiliary service, then makes the actual referral and subsequently coordinates the service as it continues so that an integrated process results. Telephone contact and in-person interviews involving the Quick Response worker, client, and auxiliary person(s) are used. Since the concrete need and the emotional experience are always related and a part of the whole, interest must extend to one as well as the other. Only through the coordination and integration of these efforts can a unified and effective service be offered.

Mrs. Truman called the agency to request legal assistance with her husband's recent abandonment of her. It was apparent to the Quick Response worker who saw her that Mrs. Truman was reacting quite intensely to multiple threats of loss; not only had her husband recently left her but she had also just undergone a mastectomy. Putting the issues in legal terms was really a thinly veiled emotional expression of anger and was aimed at revenge against her husband. Although the crisis was not a legal one, Mrs. Truman was so obsessively fixed on seeing a lawyer that the Quick Response worker evaluated it as a way of helping her move on to the more central issues. Rather than engaging in a nonproductive power struggle with Mrs. Truman as to whether the issues were legal or emotional, the worker determined it was better that they see the lawyer together. Once this had been accomplished and the displacement lessened, the significant emotional issues were more effectively confronted.

Field Activity

Whenever the worker leaves the confines of the office and is therefore away from a system that is familiar and in which he or she has a place, anxiety is inevitably heightened. The greater the worker's sense of professional self and purpose, the more discipline there will be available to tolerate this discomfort with the unknown. Even so, there must be clear theoretical underpinnings and strong structural supports to counteract a natural inclination to do what is most comfortable. Recognition that systems intervention can be more economical in terms of time and that it can accomplish what is otherwise impossible helps to support professional judgements that favor field activity. Worker and unit time have to be evaluated on some basis other than number of interviews; the amount of time spent in the field should be an important consideration in evaluation of productivity. Rather than creating adverse pressure when a worker schedules field visits, case analysis should be used to appropriately support this direction. In fact, attention should be paid to those periods when an individual worker or the unit shows a marked decrease in this activity.

Field activity is arbitrarily divided here into home visits and other systems activity because of certain characteristics unique to the former. Since the worker's schedule is open except for telephone/walk-in coverage, field visits are scheduled when indicated by simply blocking out the necessary amount of time.

HOME VISIT.   This is appropriate at any point in the Quick Response sequence and can encompass a portion or even the whole of it.

Mrs. Simms called to request marital counseling and since her husband was homebound, a home visit was arranged so that both could be involved. Home visits continued throughout the Quick Response sequence.

Mrs. Jones requested help for her mother who had been very depressed because of the father's recent death. Since it was still the official mourning period and the mother did not want to leave her house, a home visit was scheduled to include Mrs. Jones and her mother.

Treatment may develop in such a way that a home visit is indicated during the middle of the sequence.

Mr. Davis originally called about his only son, age 22, who refused to leave his room and was increasingly slovenly and hostile in his demeanor. After three office appointments with Mr. and Mrs. Davis, a home visit was arranged because they were more able to take responsibility for their part in the problem and could now participate more fully in helping their son.

Mrs. Price maintained that a good deal of the problem with her two teenaged daughters resulted from the neighborhood in which they lived. During the same time period, an aunt telephoned twice to report her sister's neglect of the children, citing hazardous conditions within the home as an important factor. A home visit was arranged for the second appointment and Mrs. Price, the daughters, and the aunt were all present.

During the home visit the family is in its own physical locale surrounded by the stage and props that are a part of their living environment. The trip from the office to the home is for the worker a journey from the familiar to the unknown, where the worker is the outsider and everyone else belongs. Family life is reflected in the home with a particular intensity and sharpness, and the situation is thus filled with new information and stimulation. The pressure to respond in a conforming way to the expectations of the family system and to take a place syntonic with its operation increases under these circumstances. The force of the family interactions and communications, coupled with the impact of the physical setting and this temporary sense of dislocation, makes the beginning of any home visit difficult. Skill is required to maintain a differentiated professional self and develop a clear therapeutic purpose.

The home visit is important because it enables workers to reach many clients who may otherwise be excluded from service, provides valuable information not obtainable in the office, and also "changes the vantage point of the data collector."

(Auerswald, 1969, p. 375) Better solutions are developed when the problem is viewed in a broader and less distorted way. Once the client has been helped to work out the problem where it naturally exists, the need to transpose a solution from the office to someplace else is avoided.

OTHER SYSTEMS ACTIVITY.   "Techniques of producing therapeutic change can be brought to arenas much larger than the therapy room or even the home."(Auerswald, 1969, p. 377) An expansion of the confines of the problem to include "an analysis of the structure of the field" necessitates exploration into different subsystems of the client's world. Very often the crisis is such that the narrower and more limited boundaries of the office exclude properties, and the interfaces and communication processes between these properties, that are needed to both understand and resolve the problem.

Subsystems within the client's larger ecological system include both formal and informal structures. Representative of the first are such governmental bureaucratic agencies as the Department of Welfare, the Division of Child Welfare, the Veterans' Administration, Medicaid, the Division of Vocational Rehabilitation, the Housing Authority, public schools, the police, and the courts. Other social service agencies and psychiatric clinics, nursery schools, and camps represent nongovernmental formal structures. Informal systems within the client's environment and likely to be part of the precipitating crisis are landlord and realty offices, neighborhood doctors, and the apartment building in which the client lives.

Systems intervention takes time and skill and unless both are allotted within the design of the delivery system, Quick Response therapy will not work successfully. There must be the recognition, for example, that 3 hours of systems activity used properly can save hours of office interview time and effect solutions otherwise unobtainable. Field visits, preparation, planning, and follow-up activity involve considerable time. The operational design of the delivery system therefore includes statistical accountability for these activities. In addition to being a measurement of the unit's productivity, the recording reinforces the importance of this work.

As with a home visit, systems activity can appropriately occur at any stage of the Quick Response sequence. Little preparation is possible when you are meeting the client for the first time.

Mrs. Jones, a speech therapist, telephoned to refer a family whose teenage daughter was being seen by her at the speech clinic. She was concerned that the girl's progress was being hampered by the parents' inordinate pressure on her but had not as yet introduced the referral. The Quick Response worker suggested she meet with the speech therapist and the family at the clinic and discussed how Mrs. Jones might introduce the possibility to the family. Once the appointment had been confirmed, there was little to do until the conference, when she could then begin to uncover the precipitating crisis and discern the subsystems involved in it.

Often, however, systems activity begins after the worker has met the family and uncovered the precipitating crisis. The objectives then are to analyze the structure of the relevant field, identify those properties that are contributing to the crisis, and develop an understanding of the interaction between subsystems. The next priority would be to plan and execute the shifts needed to resolve the problem. Preparation is essential in order to accomplish these objectives. Through discussion with the client and with those people in the system immediately identifiable, some knowledge about the formal and informal operations of the system can be gained. Information about the lines of authority and who in the organization has the decision-making ability is very relevant at this point. Once a meeting has been decided upon, it is crucial that all the people immediately involved with the client and those who have the authority to make commitments to certain plans of action attend. All too often a meeting is stymied because the person who has knowledge about a crucial facet of the problem is not there, or an important proposal is thwarted because the supervisor needed to approve the plan has been left out of the conference.

The outcome of an important meeting was significantly altered because a Bureau of Child Welfare supervisor had not attended. The conference included the client/family; the caseworker and supervisor from the private placement agency; the Quick Response worker and supervisor from the family service agency; and the BCW caseworker. Not until the conclusion of the meeting, when a strategy had been worked out among all participants, did the BCW worker indicate that supervisory approval was required before BCW could be committed to the plan. Not only did the information create confusion where solidarity had seemed imminent and delay further action, but since the BCW worker was the most ambivalent about the plan there was risk in leaving the communication about the process and results of the meeting to him. If the Quick Response worker who arranged the meeting had inquired who at BCW made case decisions, the supervisor's participation could have been arranged. At times preparation must even include a letter prior to the meeting to confirm everyone's attendance.

Even though a tentative plan about purpose and objectives is in order when a field visit on an active Quick Response case is made, flexibility to re-evaluate and revise is crucial because new information will emerge, perspectives will be jogged, and gaps will be filled if the systems activity is successful. Many of the techniques of intervention common to the casework process are used. The Quick Response worker observes and clarifies communications and interactional processes, evaluates resources, and tests out strategies and proposals. While some proposed solutions are consistent with accepted procedure, others may depend on channels not usually exercised and techniques such as confrontation can be used to effect agreement. Since the client is often included in the systems activity, attention must be focused on both the treatment of the client and the process of systems intervention.

In the Hernandez case presented in Chapter 3, the Quick Response worker, Mr. Sparks, determined that even though certain psychological factors were clear, a meeting at Sheryl's school would help determine the nature of her educational problem. Information about her academic skills and performances, the nature of the school's operation, and Sheryl's current place in all this could best be obtained from a school visit.

Discussion with the guidance counselor with whom Sheryl had previously met led to a decision to involve the Dean of Students. She was most influential in both the development of a student's educational program and in the assignment of all classes. The meeting therefore was to include Mrs. Hernandez, Sheryl, the Dean of Students, the guidance counselor, and Mr. Sparks.

The dean was obviously the school representative in charge and began with a general introduction about the school's operation, program objectives, and lines of responsibility. After some background information from Mrs. Hernandez and Mr. Sparks, an explanation about why the meeting had been requested focused the discussion on defining the problem at hand. This phase of the work was important in achieving an acurate definition of the problem and developing a mutual concern about it. Although everyone had some input in the process, Mr. Sparks' insistence upon expanding their view of the problem rather than prematurely closing off discussion was crucial. For example, questions about Sheryl's scores on reading and math tests that indicate grade level ability produced information that shifted the analysis of the problem. Rather than issues of motivation and study input, an evaluation by the dean concluded that Sheryl was seriously lacking in basic academic skills. Mrs. Hernandez's contribution of important information about Sheryl's early school experience and the Dean's review of her record and present class program substantiated a tentative analysis that these inadequate skills were at the center of her marginal performance.

The Quick Response worker's initial decision to involve the school and his insistence upon a thorough analysis of the problem and a fuller use of the school's resources yielded results. Once the problem was defined differently, it became clear that it was not Sheryl's "fault" but in fact she had been working overtime to do as well as she had. This contributed to an important shift in Mrs. Hernandez's view of Sheryl. Because of this meeting the school had become involved in the problem and the Dean was ready to make the full resources of her office available for working out a solution. Testing would be undertaken and the results used to develop a remedial tutoring program for Sheryl, with the understanding that

Sheryl, Mrs. Hernandez, and the Dean would work together on the solution.

After a meeting such as this, follow-up activity helps to reinforce the commitments and plans that have resulted. For example, a letter can be sent after the meeting to all parties who attended, summarizing what transpired, the status of agenda items, and each representative's agreements regarding future activity. This also provides a record in case of future need for clarification. Additionally, in case of staff turnover, this kind of letter in the client's record helps to maintain continuity of the agency's commitment.

Community Outreach

Familiarity with community resources and established relationships within the community that result from systems activity makes community outreach a natural part of the Quick Response unit. Since new applicants begin here anyway, this helps strengthen the bridge that already exists between the community and the agency. The Quick Response worker's involvement with all aspects of the agency's program, including auxiliary services, equips him or her particularly well to represent the agency.

Rather than being defined by the needs of a specific client, the purpose of an outreach program is to familiarize the community with the agency's services and to develop ways in which they can be appropriately used. The first step in developing an outreach program is to define the community to be served. Any number of factors can be used to accomplish this: geography, economics, religious considerations, age, and health, to name just a few. Only then can the facilities within this community that are relevant to the agency's work be identified. For example, a Jewish Family Service community outreach program developed for a community defined simply along geographic lines began by considering a wide variety of resources appropriate to its concerns: public and private schools; day-care centers; synagogues and churches; community council organizations; legal services; political organizations; community centers; and clubs. Since it is important from the beginning to have as specific a picture as possible about the target community, data should include socioeconomic factors, characteristics and customs of the population, ethnic origins, and household composition.

Once the community has been defined, its composition explored, and the workers designated for that specific project, the methods of outreach can be determined. Comparatively superficial efforts, such as posters advertising the agency's services placed in public facilities, take a minimum of effort but also have a minimum return. Articles placed in local newspapers explaining the services available or highlighting a particular agency program can be more effective in educating the public and making the agency's name a more familiar one. For an area with a heavy concentration of adolescents, a particularly imaginative program has been organized around drop-in sessions held in a mobile van. Sending an introductory letter, perhaps accompanied by a brochure and a fact sheet about the agency, is a traditional and effective beginning. The letter should be addressed to the designated head of the facility and/or the person who offers a complementary service. An appointment is requested to discuss more about services, and thus plans can be made for continued activity. When someone is already known at a community facility, an introduction to the appropriate person can often be arranged through them.

The introductory interview is used to exchange information about services and to determine whether there is any mutuality of purpose. If so, it is important to learn something about the structural operations of this facility and the people who staff it. Preliminary determination can be made about whether a formal relationship is feasible between the resources and, if so, involving what personnel and around what services.

As ideas regarding this determination become clearer, a second interview may be needed so as to include other significant people.

During an introductory interview at a private school, the guidance counselor expressed an interest in having an agency social worker spend half a day per week at the school. The social worker would provide direct service to children and their families when crisis intervention and/or referral work was indicated, as well as consultation services to teachers. This kind of program was both familiar and feasible to the family service agency, and thus it became an area of mutual interest. When the cost of the program was discussed, the guidance counselor suggested that the next meeting include the school's staff person responsible for the development of financial grants.

When evaluating the effect of one person being in favor and another opposed to a proposed program, the position, authority, and function of both must be considered.

The placement counselor at a large law school wanted to arrange an effective referral system with a nearby family service agency since he sometimes encountered students who needed counseling. This was especially true at stressful points such as when the demands of graduation and job hunting coincided. He had also been identified informally by the students as someone to whom they could go with a psychological problem. However, in meeting with the Dean of Students, it became clear to the community outreach worker that although he had overtly authorized the plan he did not believe in psychotherapy and was unsympathetic to students needing this kind of help. Nevertheless, even though the Dean had a senior position and more authority, the placement counselor's formal and informal position in the system meant that students would bring their problems to him. Since the Dean had officially approved, there was no reason not to arrange a working relationship between the placement counselor and the agency.

If through these preliminary meetings an interest in developing a formal arrangement emerges, a period of discussion, negotiation, and testing out will follow.

Although the setting in which Quick Response is housed influences the working relationships and programs developed, the examples that follow are appropriate to a social service agency such as Jewish Family Service and indicate the variety possible:

LIAISON ARRANGEMENT.   A Quick Response worker is designated to help determine and then facilitate all referrals between the two organizations. Effective working relationships with staffpersons at the referring resource are developed so that an ongoing mutual education process results in appropriate decisions about when and how to refer. Telephone contact and field visits are fully used. The relationship established between the law school and family agency just discussed is an example of this type of arrangement.

FAMILY LIFE EDUCATION (FLE) PROGRAM.   A time-limited educational program in an area of the agency's expertise is designed to be of interest to the population of the community resource being visited. A single event, a series of topical lectures, or a small-group discussion can be planned for the people who use the facility, for the staff, and/or for the Board. This program is often effectively combined with a liaison arrangement.

A FLE program was developed for a synagogue whose congregation had a large number of families with adolescent-aged children. Highlighted in discussion with the rabbi were these parents' concerns about increasing alienation between themselves and their children. During the year the FLE program consisted of a number of different efforts to learn more about and help with these problems. The rabbi first introduced the FLE worker to the synagogue Board and information about the agency and its services was presented. Since the Board consisted of many members who were involved in the synagogue's daily activities, their cooperation and support were important. A single-event evening was planned with a presentation entitled, "The Role of the Family in Today's Changing World."

Being more familiar with the synagogue's members, the [community outreach] worker then held an informal, less structured series of four small group discussions on "The Generation Gap? How to Talk to Your Teenagers; How to Talk to Your Parents."

CONSULTATION PROGRAM.   Here the worker must maintain an identity as a representative of the primary agency while functioning as an integral part of the other setting. A consultation service offers use of the agency's expertise by and at the other facility on a regular ongoing basis. Consultation programs are especially applicable in settings such as community centers and schools. The program presented earlier between the private school and a family service agency exemplifies this arrangement. Since this is a time-consuming project, careful consideration has to be given regarding whether a Quick Response worker will staff it.

Community outreach is a complex endeavor that requires know-how and time to accomplish effectively. Many skills used in Quick Response treatment—such as a focused evaluation, use of time, determination of focus and agreement, along with methods of family and systems intervention—are used in outreach work. Time is needed to maintain active programs, to follow up on certain previously contacted resources, and to develop new outreach efforts.

GROUP PHENOMENA

The construction of a unit to deliver Quick Response service, as well as the coordination of different kinds of activity within that unit, creates a connection and interplay among the workers that fosters a strong group identity. The sharing of telephone/walk-in coverage, the importance of information distribution about community resources and health and welfare policies, joint efforts on community outreach, and the general need for a more active and present-oriented professional stance, all contribute to the creation of a group that maximizes the worker's independence and encourages help from colleagues, while minimizing the traditional hierarchical dependence.

Certain aspects of providing Quick Response service can be difficult: the unpredictability of telephone/walk-in reception; continuous beginnings with people in crisis; the mix of cases in any Quick Response caseload that necessitates variation in modes of intervention; and the frequency of beginnings and endings. A sense of a shared experience helps to strengthen the group's cohesiveness and to translate a supportive attitude into productive action.

In order to help other workers learn about and keep abreast of the policies and procedures of public health and welfare services, a Quick Response worker voluntarily compiled a manual about eligibility requirements, application and review procedures, and special services of agencies such as the Department of Social Services, Medicaid, and food stamps. Periodically she taught a course on this for new workers and a refresher session for the more experienced ones.

Further examples of ways in which group support can be channeled into constructive activity are the development of a buddy system to assist new workers in learning certain Quick Response tasks, and a pairing system used between workers as a vehicle for peer case consultation and exchange on selected professional issues. Group supervision, to be discussed in Chapter 5, also has a significant impact on group process.

Within any Quick Response unit there will be variations as to the kind and amount of professional experience. Some workers will be more ready for increased leadership responsibility than others, so variation in learning opportunities within the unit is therefore important. Some community outreach assignments, for example, are more demanding of leadership skills than others and can be assigned accordingly. Volunteers who work on the processing of health and welfare assistance applications need training and supervision; this provides an excellent opportunity for a beginning introduction to supervisory issues. Social work graduate students have been successfully placed in the Quick Response unit when a worker is ready for more supervisory responsibility. The richness of a Quick Response unit stems, in part, from the wide range of opportunities for professional growth and development inherently possible within the work of the unit.

THE UNIT AS A SUBSYSTEM

Although a Quick Response unit is a complex system, it is also a subsystem of a larger organization such as a social service agency, mental health facility, hospital, court, or school. In a family service agency such as Jewish Family Service, where all cases begin in Quick Response and the largest percentage of cases within the agency at any given time are being seen in Quick Response, the unit's operations are central to the functioning of the larger system. However, whatever the setting and Quick Response's place in it, attention to the operations of the overall system, to interactions between the unit and other subsystems, and to the effect on the whole of changes within the unit, constitutes a continuously important process.

Chapter 5

THE TEACHING AND SUPERVISION
OF QUICK RESPONSE

TRAINING ISSUES

There is usually a wide variety of reactions to the introduction of a Quick Response service and first impressions are heavily influenced by the practitioner's previous training and experience. While it is natural to want to translate new concepts into familiar terms, premature comparisons are often made even when knowledge is limited. Fantasies about changes are used to try to predict future developments. Even though beginning reactions will vary depending on the nature of previous intellectual and emotional investments, blanket acceptance or rejection is equally insubstantial at this early point. The introduction of any new psychotherapy invariably stimulates ambivalences and, therefore, a strong administrative commitment to Quick Response is important. Mann (1973) points out that

> it is usually insufficient to introduce a new treatment method,
> particularly if it incorporates some unusual innovations, by

proposing that it be tried in a modest way and given the test of
application and outcome. The emotional resistances to it are
apt to foreclose a fair trial since it will seem in the best personal
interests of those so involved to make certain it will fail. (pp.
78–79)

As part of any beginning phase of learning, receptivity
must be heightened so that new ideas are met with interest and
curiosity rather than premature judgements. Comparisons
may persist but competitive elements have to be lessened. An
opportunity to react openly to the material as it is presented
and to explore biased views is important, because learning
depends upon a certain freedom from predetermined positions
and a readiness to listen, hear, and try what is being presented.
A group format such as a supervisory group or a seminar can
be especially helpful at this early stage. What one person is
hesitant to say, another will risk; and when one side is presented, the opposite inevitably emerges.

To learn any form of psychotherapy requires more than
abstract understanding. Ideas come to life and take form only
when put into practice, and the emotional issues central to the
practitioner's effectiveness are activated most critically when
real people and real crises are presented. Significant issues are
formulated, confronted, and learned when theory and practice
are combined. With adequate supervision the worker can
move into practice fairly early in the learning process. Difficulties predictably arise around the more innovative aspects of
Quick Response and the practitioner needs help with both the
tasks to be mastered and the emotional issues involved. These
many challenges during this beginning period advise against
trying to learn another treatment method simultaneously.

Availability and Quick Response

Time in Quick Response treatment is arranged to decrease artificial delays in service, and field activity moves the

practitioner more quickly into the client's environment and away from the familiarity of the office. This can heighten anxieties about the unknown and compound the conflict between wanting to help and being afraid of getting overly involved. As part of many traditional intake procedures, the client is subtly instructed how to behave and a facade of predictability is arranged. Quick Response entails less of this element; it attempts to meet the client more in his or her own time and environment. Instead of safeguarding against surprises and uncertainty, the worker is thrust more forcefully into what is unknown. Usually those new to Quick Response readily agree intellectually with the principles but underestimate what they mean in practice. Anxieties and discomforts about proceeding in such a situation emerge when workers are actually faced with the emotional demands of the tasks. Rather than an appropriate sense of what has to be uncertain at this beginning point, exaggerated expectations and omnipotent fantasies of what the worker thinks he or she should know interfere with movement into the unpredictable situation and make it seem inordinately risky. When the worker is also inexperienced and has little confidence in any treatment process, the risk seems greater and failure more likely.

Unless this conflict is confronted, workers often attempt to deal with these external and internal demands by distancing and delaying involvement with the client. Although on the surface it may seem as if the worker is available to meet the client, the more subtle message is of hedging and delay: Even though the client expresses a willingness, even an eagerness on the telephone to make an appointment, the worker persists in questioning her about herself, the situation, and even the precipitating crisis; tasks are set up for the client to do before a first appointment can be arranged; decisions are made prematurely about what services are available. Often unaware of this self-protective behavior, the worker rationalizes the procedures used. Naturally, as part of the learning process the conflictual activity must be recognized, the ambivalences dealt with more productively, and intellectual and emotional readiness made more compatible.

Treatment Focus and Time Limit

When the concepts of a time limit and treatment focus are introduced, there is usually considerable objection. The six-session limitation on time provokes the more intense reaction even though many of the same underlying issues are involved in the resistances to one as to the other. Disagreement is usually voiced on theoretical grounds, but those dynamic issues of separation/loss, adequacy/inadequacy, and independence/dependence aroused in the client also pertain to the practitioner. However, discussion never begins with an acknowledgement of this and learning will be blocked if resistances are not understood and dealt with for what they are.

The need for more time to build a trusting relationship; reflections on the complexities of individual, family, and systems problems; and the difficulty of unraveling a pathological relationship of long standing, are all cited as reasons for objecting to the time limit and treatment focus. Mann (1973) details further,

> He will find the selection of a central issue interesting, but too restrictive to expect that concentration on the one issue can lead to any kind of satisfying resolution. He will not believe that it will be possible for an intense transference situation to develop so rapidly, nor will he believe that the dynamic events can appear so clearly and so swiftly. It will follow logically in his thinking that this being so, it would hardly be likely that the termination period could induce a powerful reaction in the patient and be a powerful instrument for resolution for both patient and therapist. (p. 79)

Although much of this may have merit if related to other forms of psychotherapy, it ignores the conceptual base of Quick Response: uncovering the precipitating crisis, defining a treatment focus, and establishing a time-limited framework. The speed with which brief is equated with less, quantity with quality, indicates the extent of the investment in this position and the intensity of the threat inherent in the presentation of another possibility. Concerns about separation constitute the underlying threat. If there is no tangible point of termination, work can remain unlimited in time and purpose, separation distant and unreal. There can always be more to do: evaluations can be delayed and omnipotent fantasies can persist unchallenged. If, however, time is limited from the beginning and treatment is focused, then the point of separation and the goals to be accomplished are very explicit. Any conflictual feelings the practitioner has around separation, adequacy, and dependency are activated.

The crisis nature of the client's entry into treatment, the practitioner's availability, and their commonality of purpose all contribute to a more intense relationship than might ordinarily be expected. When coupled with the intensification of the transference that is stimulated by the time limit, the relationship proves to be a significant one. If the worker has difficulty with the simultaneous fact of separation, he may attempt to minimize the impact of the relationship and thus diffuse its potential. If the worker's omnipotent fantasies are stimulated by the client's dependent feelings, the worker may distort the client's need for him or her, as well as his or her own need to be the nurturer. Separation may be actively denied or compromised and this information communicated to the client. On the other hand, the time-limited structure of Quick Response can also be used by the worker as an excuse for distancing and protecting himself or herself from whatever dependency feelings are aroused. Neither way works, of course, because the time-limited and treatment-focused nature of Quick Response continually tests real feelings and adaptations to the issues of separation/loss, independence/dependence.

At times those new to Quick Response inappropriately

emphasize behavorial changes and demand evidence that gains are being made. The more dynamic and affective aspects of a problem are avoided and regressive behavior is not tolerated. These attempts to maintain distance from the client may also indicate a preoccupation with the evaluation that is a part of separation. If conflicts around questions of adequacy are heightened and the worker feels put on the line, she or he may in turn put the client on the line to perform. If the decision about termination is usually experienced by the worker as a source of power and this fans the flame of omnipotent fantasies, the opposite side of the conflict may emerge when it is taken out of his control. (Mann, 1973, p. 80) The review and evaluation connected with separation threaten to expose the worker's fantasied inadequacies so that he or she can no longer see it in realistic terms.

These resistances and conflicts about specific aspects of Quick Response only become apparent if the training process carries a clear and consistent expectation regarding the execution of these principles. Only then can the resistances be recognized and dealt with appropriately.

Frequency of Beginnings and Endings

Carrying a full Quick Response caseload multiplies the frequency of beginnings and endings, and the worker often begins and ends with more than one client/family at a time. Unless the emotional conflicts that are often intensified when doing Quick Response are recognized and understood, not only will attempts be made to circumvent these processes, but the work will be experienced as inordinately stressful. If the demands of availability and quick involvement continually evoke fears around merging and loss of individuation, then constant beginnings are going to take an emotional toll. When separation is experienced solely as a loss and too often provokes feelings of inadequacy, then numerous endings with no sense of closure and satisfaction will be depleting. Energy used self-protectively leaves less energy available for learning, so the work becomes exhausting. However, since anyone new to Quick Response experiences some stimulation of unresolved conflicts and testing of adaptive mechanisms, heightened anxiety during the beginning period is common. Opportunities must be allowed within the training process for adequate discussion of these dynamic issues so that the worker is made aware of what is happening. While it is necessary to allow for individual differences, there is sufficient universality in the questions at hand that group reflection can be supportive and constructive in helping the worker move less defensively and be more available to learn.

Integration of Concrete and Psychological Services

Since Quick Response therapy considers the client-problem-situation on a continuum that includes the ecological, family, and individual systems, intervention in more than one arena at a time is entirely consistent and any artificial division between concrete services, psychological counseling, and systems intervention is counterindicated. The practitioner used to working with the client in a singular vein sometimes finds this difficult and resistance takes various forms: Psychological issues are avoided when concrete services are given; intrapsychic phenomona are considered extraneous to advocacy work; concrete services are viewed outside of family dynamics. Realistically, a treatment plan that includes intervention on several levels at a time is more complex and demands flexibility. However, resistance to a broader based approach lies also in the fact that the practitioner's authority position is more exposed when concrete services are considered. Although authority issues emerge in any treatment relationship, they are heightened and obvious when transactions involve the approval or disapproval, providing or not providing of financial assistance, homemaker services, visiting nurse care, tutoring programs, and camp scholarships. Consequently, feelings and perceptions about this authority become more pronounced and the worker's discomfort increases as her or his omnipotent fantasies and distortions about the meaning of this responsibility are stimulated. In reaction, the worker may attempt to create distance from the client's emotional life and depersonalize the situation. The power and responsibility of the decision-making process are minimized or negated by simply functioning as a conduit between the client's request and the supervisor's decision, transmitting the message without appraisal or evaluation. On the other hand, the practitioner may act as if he or she knows it all, requiring no information or explanation from the client, excluding the client from the process and operating omnipotently.

Case discussion regarding the interrelationships of concrete needs, systems phenomena, and psychological issues as facets of the client's problem helps those new to Quick Response to understand why, when, and how they must be included in the Quick Response treatment. Increased understanding about the complexity with which precipitating crises evolve and are expressed makes it easier to determine one's place in the picture. This perspective helps diminish omnipotent fantasies and allows the client's needs to move into the foreground so that a more balanced view can emerge.

Countertransference Reactions and Quick Response

In addition to these predictable points of emotional resistance typical for those new to Quick Response, countertransference reactions are as much a part of this practice as they are of any psychotherapy. "[U]nder certain conditions he [the worker], like the client, will unconsciously transfer into his relationships certain positive or negative reactions that are realistically uncalled for." (Perlman, 1957, p. 81) Contrary to long-term treatment, the Quick Response time limit prevents a continuation of the case in a nonproductive yet nonending cycle because of a countertransference bind. On the other hand, the crisis orientation and quick involvement sometimes intensifies countertransference reactions more than might otherwise be expected. Professional efforts such as self-reflection, supervision, and consultation are needed to handle them in order not to limit the client's progress. The shortness of treatment time makes a swift and disciplined identification especially important and awareness of typical trends in one's own subjective reactions facilitate this. Supervision is essential in helping the new practitioner develop this critical self-awareness.

SUPERVISION AND QUICK RESPONSE

Quick Response can be taught in workshops, seminars, and classrooms, but the supervisory process that is part of a work experience usually provides a more concentrated and continued opportunity for teaching and learning. Any introduction of Quick Response should begin with an explanation about its purpose and rationale and some reflection on the historical factors that contributed to its development. An understanding of the unit's place in the overall operations of the facility within which it exists contributes to a better appreciation of Quick Response's part in providing effective service. These factors usually have a positive impact on the practitioner's desire to learn, and they also help to foster a more receptive attitude.

All teaching material and methods commonly used in supervision can be used in teaching Quick Response: study of theory, case presentation, process recording, role-playing, taped interviews, and direct observation of live interviews. The latter is a valuable but unfortunately underemployed way of teaching any psychotherapy since it demonstrates for the student just what is to be done. Preparation before and discussion after each viewed interview are equally important if the most is to be gained. Because of its briefness, Quick Response is especially well suited for observation from beginning to end. One aspect of the treatment, such as uncovering the precipitating crisis or introducing the treatment agreement, can also be singled out for observation in a number of cases. In general, however, different teaching methods should be used simultaneously. For example, even though the worker observes as the supervisor interviews a Quick Response case, the worker's own cases still need the attention that process recording and case discussion provide.

Since Quick Response treatment is brief and tasks have a general order to them, it is usually clear when a problem develops: A home visit is not offered on telephone reception when clearly indicated; the precipitating crisis remains uncovered; the treatment focus is undeveloped or unclear; the time limit is not introduced or is presented ambiguously; a treatment agreement is vague or not sought after; systems activity is incomplete; mixed messages are given about ending. If the supervisor plans an interview carefully with the worker so that the worker has a clear and definite idea of its purpose, followup discussion can determine if and how it was accomplished. When problems are evident, their nature has to be properly diagnosed: Were the dynamics of the case understood? Are the skills needed to execute the task within the practitioner's grasp? Are resistances to that particular facet of the treatment operating? Carlotte Towle wrote in 1954 on the theory of learning in social work:

> When we characterize the individual's efforts to survive as "defenses," aggression essential to master learning may be referred to as a defense against feeling inadequate rather than as an aspect of the individual's characteristic learning pattern. . . . [W]hen an individual accepts the new with some reservation, questioning it, analyzing it, breaking it down into bits to reflect upon, . . . actually he is busily engaged in incorporating changes." (pp. 128-129)

As previously discussed, however, there are predictable points of resistance typical for someone new to Quick Response that also cause difficulty with incorporating new information. The supervisor must correctly determine the problem and pinpoint where the student is in the learning process before knowing what is needed to move forward.

Group and Individual Supervision

Supervision can be conducted individually and in groups. Although each has certain advantages, group supervision is particularly well suited to a Quick Response service because it parallels much of Quick Response activity: Clients are often seen in family groups; systems intervention includes group meetings; and the service operates as a unit or group. It provides an opportunity for the practitioner to become familiar with functioning professionally in such a setting and to learn about group dynamics. Discussion of therapeutic material in a group, and the openness and exposure involved in presenting one's own and discussing others' case material sensitize the practitioner to parallels in the treatment situation. Dynamics such as interactional phenomena, leadership and authority relationships, alliances and pairing, and group crises are all paradigmatic of the treatment situation. Just as some of the unit's operations depend upon shared tasks and responsibility, so the functioning of a supervisory group depends upon the full participation of its members in such activities as case presentation and discussion, consideration of theoretical issues, and dealing with questions of agenda.

Group supervision supports the worker's active and independent functioning, which is all-important in Quick Response. Participation in one's own and others' case presentations and the integration of this information into practice is an active process. Conceptual skills improve when ideas have to be ordered, formulated, and clarified so that others understand them. Since the intensity of the hierarchical relationship in individual supervision is lessened when the learning is distributed among a number of relationships, regressive elements resulting from a more concentrated dependency on the supervisor are minimized. The opportunity to depend upon peers as well as the supervisor, being in both the teaching and learning role, and observing peers doing likewise serve to enhance self-esteem and to reinforce an autonomous professional self.

Weekly group supervision should be supplemented with some individual supervision, the amount to be determined by both the individual's professional level of functioning and her or his knowledge of Quick Response. This arrangement can be especially helpful to the worker first beginning in Quick Response, since in addition to learning a new treatment modality he or she has to become familiar with many agency forms and procedures. Unless other supervisory group members are also new, there will inevitably be a gap that individual attention can fill between the group agenda and what has to be known right away. Also, individual supervision is necessary when work with the practitioner, new or otherwise, involves the planning and follow-up of each interview throughout a case. Finally, the identification of individual learning patterns can be either a group or an individual supervisory function. As a group develops, supervisory leadership is used to encourage, focus, and confront the group so that this kind of individuation is taken on as a group responsibility. The maturity of the supervisory group will influence whether individual supervision is needed for this work.

The Quick Response Supervisor

Supervision of a Quick Response unit includes a regulatory and evaluative function as well as the function of teaching. Decisions about such matters as case disposition, resource allocation, program planning, schedules, and work assignments regulate the activity of each worker and the unit as a whole. The supervisor evaluates the practitioner's work performance and that of the overall operations of the unit in terms of agency standards and expectations. The successful integration of these functions within the supervisory relationship is crucial to the professional development of the worker and to the productive functioning of the unit.

The cohesiveness of the Quick Response unit depends upon strong leadership; to provide this, the Quick Response supervisor must know and care about what transpires on a daily basis, as well as being concerned with the more general flow of the unit. Crucial to the creation and maintenance of a productive group process is a leader capable of determining when to rely upon and encourage group problem solving and decision making and when the responsibility rests more solely in his or her hands. The stability that comes from positive leadership encourages growth in the practitioner and confidence in the group.

The nature of Quick Response does not allow for delay or postponement; consequently, the supervisor must be actively involved in the daily operations of the unit and available in ways that are unique to Quick Response. The continual flow of cases, the crisis orientation of the service, the availability at point of application, and the time-limited nature of the treatment are just a few of the reasons the supervisor must constantly keep in touch with the status of the operation. For example, since the effective functioning of telephone/walk-in coverage is so central to Quick Response, the supervisor must be alert to difficulties when they arise. The supervisor who is cognizant of what is happening can quickly move to remedy problems that may occur when workers are out sick or overloaded. Supervisory involvement also reinforces the importance of these activities.

The supervisor realistically and paradigmatically must be available to the worker at times without delay, just as the worker is for the client. Her or his help is sometimes needed immediately in crisis situations such as evictions, suicide threats, and violence between family members; and often, concrete assistance such as financial aid requires immediate approval. In a similar vein, the systems intervention and field activity of Quick Response often necessitates the supervisor's direct involvement alongside the worker. Not only is the learning of systems intervention facilitated by the supervisor's participation in real situations, but often his or her authority and expertise are needed. Also, if a meeting requires a supervisor from another agency to attend, both protocol and practicality usually demand that the complementary agency person be present. Not only is learning facilitated by the supervisor's participation in community outreach, but his or her authority is often necessary at selected points in the process of negotiating broader agency commitments of this kind. In order to prevent this process from becoming overly long or burdensome, the Quick Response supervisor needs either the authority to finalize community outreach arrangements or a direct line to the person who can.

The introduction of Quick Response frequently provokes a range of responses from interest to suspicion; since the unit works closely with many other services within the agency and in the community, it is important that the purpose, rationale, and methods of Quick Response be correctly understood. The comprehensive use of auxiliary services, as well as the transfer and referral of cases, renders indispensable good working relationships based upon correct perceptions of respective services. Therefore, the Quick Response supervisor must function in an educational, liaison, and public relations capacity both intra- and interagency, in order to properly explain the service, correct misinformation, and establish the kind of relationships and procedures that foster joint efforts beneficial to the client.

Administrative Function of the Quick Response Supervisor

Administrative responsibility involves the establishment of new principles and the development of the policies and procedures that put them into practice. During any period of change, new ground is constantly being broken and some of the old has to be updated or replaced. Because Quick Response usually reflects some change in direction, administrative considerations are relevant to many aspects of the unit's functioning. Questions about policy and procedure and their adaptation to practice are raised in connection with such issues as case disposition, allocation of time, organizational design of telephone/walk-in coverage, direction of community outreach, and evaluation of systems activities. Regardless whether the Quick Response supervisor's role is limited to the effecting of new policies and procedures already established by administration, or whether he or she has a direct part in the making of these decisions, the newness of Quick Response and the impact of changes resulting from its inception make a direct channel of communication between the Quick Response supervisor and the administration very important.

Chapter 6

OTHER SETTINGS IN WHICH
QUICK RESPONSE CAN BE USED

Quick Response developed from a recognition that to better serve the population typical to a family agency, updated concepts about when, where, and how people need help had to be integrated into practice. Even though innovative forms of treatment are being developed and offered today at social service and mental health facilities throughout the country, many agencies still have not incorporated these concepts into practice. There is often a delay for an intake appointment and then clients are put on a waiting list for continued services. The current aspects of the client's disequilibrium are minimized and the natural limits on time are insufficiently considered. Office-centered service negates the importance of the client's ecological system in the present dysfunction. The client's problem is still too often categorized as either concrete or psychological. Although newer projects are more often designed to make use of updated concepts, the mainstream of service takes longer to change. The Quick Response service is especially important because it was developed for use with the majority of clients who seek help from a social service agency, yet it recognizes and leaves room for those clients who need and can use other services.

Quick Response's broad applicability to a wide range of health, welfare, educational, and legal settings makes it an even more valuable service. In addition to social service and mental health agencies, hospitals, schools, placement facilities, and courts are all settings in which it has a place. Social workers, psychologists, psychiatrists, marriage counselors, doctors, nurses, guidance counselors, child welfare workers, and court workers will all find it applicable to much of their work.

Settings with Time Limit

Many practitioners work in settings where time is externally limited, either because of the nature of the setting, the defined role of the professional person within that setting, and/or problems attributable to understaffing. Therefore, a treatment modality that conceives of time dynamically and has integrated its natural limits into the treatment structure holds enormous potential.

Hospital care is one example where the available treatment time is limited by the circumstances that bring the recipient for help. Since many patients stay for only a short period of time, the social worker's, nurse's, and doctor's involvement with the patient is also time-limited. For those individuals and families who need help coping with the disequilibrium that occurs prior to hospitalization, the stay itself, or the planning for post-hospitalization, Quick Response allows the time-limited nature of both the hospitalization and the crisis to be considered together. Time is recognized and used from the beginning as a positive and integral aspect of the help offered: treatment has a beginning, middle, and end phase; a focus is established, an agreement made, and goals accomplished. This encourages all who are involved to take an active part in the course of events rather than to subtly support a passive stance.

There are numerous other settings where this pattern applies. For example, the individual and family crisis that is precipitated by and reflected in court proceedings such as juvenile arrests, divorce, and custody petitions often indicates the need for psychosocial intervention. The sequence of legal events, however, externally limits the treatment time available. Another example is that of the school system, in which the guidance counselor's work is often time-limited because of both his or her role within the system and frequent problems with understaffing.

Settings with Crisis Potential

When factors of illness, separation, and loss come into play, usual coping mechanisms are put under considerable stress; for those who are unable to handle this, help is needed. The stresses at points of application, admission to and discharge from health and welfare facilities often contribute to a crisis. Such settings include, for example, hospitals, placement facilities, services to the aged and even public assistance programs. When Quick Response is appropriately used at these points, the capacity for helping the client/family re-establish an equilibrium and possibly improve their adaptive resources can also contribute to better use of the facility's services. Examples are innumerable: a family member's admission to or discharge from a nursing home, rehabilitation center, or hospital; pre- or postoperation or diagnosis of serious illness; application of a family member for public assistance or unemployment insurance; initiation of legal proceedings related to an arrest, divorce, or custody questions.

Settings That Require a Systems Approach

Since Quick Response views the individual/family in the context of its ecological system and places importance upon its interaction with the operations of larger bureaucratic organizations, it can be used in settings where a systems approach is crucial to effective service. This applies when work with the client involves such large and complex systems as schools, hospitals, placement facilities, and public welfare programs. For example, when trying to determine the nature of a sudden problem with one of the children at a day care center, the social worker needed to explore the home and family situation, the system in operation at the day care center, and the interaction of both. Relationships within the classroom, a recent meeting between the director and parents, the family's feeling about the center were just a few of the possible factors that may have contributed to the crisis. The systems approach central to Quick Response provides a framework within which to evaluate these factors and a method for effective intervention.

Naturally, in many of these settings, more than one and even all three of the following components can be present: (1) Crisis factors are inherent in the conditions that bring the client there; (2) limitation of time is a given; and (3) systems factors are operative. For example, use of a Quick Response approach allows the hospital social worker to offer help immediately when the client/family's disequilibrium is identified, to pace service to coincide whth the time-limited nature of the hospitalization, and to provide a basis for both the hospital and family systems to be considered part of treatment. The integration of concrete and psychological services further helps the client/family resolve the crisis.

Settings That Offer Long-Term Care

Quick Response can also be used by many health and welfare organizations whose primary function involves long-term care: child-welfare agencies that provide foster care and residential treatment; facilities for the chronically ill, aged, and handicapped; as well as psychiatric hospitals. Reid and Epstein (1972), in *Task-Centered Casework*, distinguish between the caseworker's maintenance and treatment functions in these settings. Brief therapy is suggested for those psychosocial problems that arise especially at points of "critical transition." (pp. 201–203) The practitioner who has ongoing case responsibility does not have the flexibility of time to offer Quick Response treatment, but once he or she has determined this need, a Quick Response worker can intervene. If the regular worker is not expected to tax what is usually an already busy schedule, and in fact sees Quick Response as an appropriate solution, that worker will be more likely to expedite the referral.

The uniqueness of Quick Response is how it integrates an increased responsiveness to the client's request for help and present crisis, an expanded use of family and systems factors, and a time-limited treatment structure. Its applicability to such a wide range of settings further substantiates the potential and significance of this service. Quick Response is an exciting and effective form of brief therapy that many human service professionals will find helpful to use.

REFERENCES

Ackerman, N. *Treating the troubled family.* New York: Basic Books, 1966.

Auerswald, E. Interdisciplinary versus ecological approach. In W. Gray, F. Duhl, & N. Rizzo (Eds.), *General systems theory and psychiatry.* Boston: Little, Brown, 1969.

Beck, D. F. *Patterns in use of family agency service.* New York: Family Service Association of America, 1962.

Bertalanffy, L. V. An overview. In W. Gray, F. Duhl, & N. Rizzo (Eds.), *General systems theory and psychiatry.* Boston: Little, Brown, 1969.

Caplan, G. *Principles of preventive psychiatry.* New York: Basic Books, 1964.

Gray, W., Duhl, F., & Rizzo, N. *General systems theory and psychiatry.* Boston: Little, Brown, 1969.

Golan, N. *Treatment in crisis situations.* New York: The Free Press, 1978.

Hoffman, D., & Remmel, M. Uncovering the precipitant in crisis intervention. *Social Casework,* 1975, *56* (5), 259–267.

Johnston, Becky. The development of Quick Response units in the Jewish Family Service. Unpublished manuscript, 1971.

Kaufman, M. Short-term family therapy. In H. Parad (Ed.), *Crisis intervention.* New York: Family Service Association of America, 1965.

Lang, J. Planned short-term treatment in a family agency. *Social Casework,* 1974, *55* (6), 369–374.

135

Mann, J. *Time-limited psychotherapy*. Cambridge, Mass.: Harvard University Press, 1973.

Parad, H. *Crisis intervention*. New York: Family Service Association of America, 1965.

Parad, H. Preventive casework: Problems and implications. In H. Parad (Ed.), *Crisis intervention*. New York: Family Service Association of America, 1965.

Parad, H., & Caplan, G. A framework for studying families in Crisis. In H. Parad (Ed.), *Crisis intervention*. New York: Family Service Association of America, 1965.

Parad H., & Parad, L. A study of crisis-oriented planned short-term treatment: Part I. *Social Casework*, 1968, *49* (6), 346–355.

Parad, L., & Parad, H. Study of crisis-oriented planned short-term treatment: Part II. *Social Casework*, 1968, *49* (7), 418–426.

Perlman, H. H. *Social casework*. Chicago: University of Chicago Press, 1957.

Perlman, H. H. Some notes on the waiting-list. In H. Parad (Ed.), *Crisis intervention*. New York: Family Service Association of America, 1965.

Rapoport, L. Crisis-oriented short-term casework. *Social Service Review*, 1967, *41* (1), 31–43.

Rapoport, L. The state of crisis: Some theoretical considerations. In H. Parad (Ed.), *Crisis intervention*. New York: Family Service Association of America, 1965.

Rapoport, L. Working with families in crisis: An exploration in preventive intervention. In H. Parad (Ed.), *Crisis intervention*. New York: Family Service Association of America, 1965.

Reid, W., & Epstein, L. *Task centered casework*. New York: Columbia University Press, 1972.

Rosenberg, B. Planned short term treatment in developmental crisis. *Social Casework*, 1975, *56* (4), 195–204.

Stein, I. *Systems theory, science, and social work*. Metuchen, N.J.: Scarecrow Press, 1974.

Stein, I. The systems model and social systems theory: Their application to casework. In H. Strean (Ed.), *Social casework: Theories in action*. Metuchen, N.J.: Scarecrow Press, 1971.

Strean, H. S. *Clinical social work: Theory and practice*. New York: The Free Press, 1978.

Towle, C. *The learner in education for the professions*. Chicago: University of Chicago Press, 1954.

INDEX